TABLE OF CONTENTS

Jennifer Bardot

Struggle and Strength

It's 1993.

I'm in the third grade.

My academic performance evaluation comes home with a report from the special education teacher. The verdict: My reading, writing, and comprehension skills are all poor. I won't keep up with school. I need to be put on an IEP (Individualized Education Program) because I have been diagnosed with a "Learning Disability." I will never graduate from high school.

My self-esteem was low, and I couldn't understand why my friends didn't have these same struggles. Making friends came easily, but school seemed impossible. As a nine-year-old, recess was the highlight of my day, and getting pulled from it to sit in a "resource lab" for additional instruction was discouraging. I despised being associated with the word "disability." I felt like a liability. I did not want to ask for help or special accommodation. I kept quiet, not even wanting my teachers or peers to know my struggles. I didn't think they could possibly understand. How could they? They were miles ahead of me. But I had to keep going and forge my path.

My family's work ethic has always been strong—and when my mom asked me, "Did you give it your all?", I could leave no doubt that I did.

I worked twice as hard as my peers, spending many hours after school with a private reading tutor, but I still felt like I wasn't enough. I had to hold myself accountable and be honest with myself, and that meant being vulnerable and exploring alternative paths. For me to find success, that meant leaning on a peer for support. I can laugh about it now, but I probably never failed a grade because of a friend I made in the first grade who would help me regularly. Julie is still a good friend today, and this is a prime example of how belief and support matter! (Thank you, Jewels!)

In the years following, I had many subsequent evaluations and IQ assessments which consistently indicated I was smart—above average, in fact. But if I was smart, why did I *still* struggle so much with seemingly simple things like reading, writing, and testing? I asked myself this over the next three decades, and I'm glad I kept asking the question. At the age of thirty-eight, I've discovered that I have dyslexia. This epiphany gives me answers now, but as I look back I realize that this unknown impairment forever shaped my character to be resilient, to build strength, and to push through "the hard" to blaze new pathways to figure things out. Resilience enabled a C student in grade school to make the Dean's List in graduate school.

I now also see that my resilience has changed over time. When I was a child, my motivation to be resilient came from wanting to blend in. As an adult, my motivation comes from accepting the challenges brought by my dyslexia as rare gifts—gifts that have forced me to approach things from unique angles. My motivators are no longer fear and shame but are now grace and acceptance. This is my journey of resilience (and I'm still on it). I'll never outgrow my disability, but my commitment to "doing my best" is my guiding light to avoid becoming another statistic.

I shared this story in my first chapter in *Owning Your G.R.I.T.* Many of us who are diagnosed with unseen disabilities may feel the same as I did: filled with self-doubt, shame, or feeling like you don't fit in. When people with disabilities are marginalized and underestimated, our society misses out on their skills and talents. Many people with disabilities pay higher out-of-pocket health care costs and are more likely to live below the federal poverty level than those without disabilities; but on the flip side many extremely successful entrepreneurs have disabilities, e.g., Richard Branson, Oprah Winfrey, Jim Carrey, and Albert Einstein to name a few of my favorites.

I hope sharing these facts provides an inclusive employment opportunity for all to contribute and change these statistics. It takes courage to own a disability, and it took me till now to openly admit I have dyslexia. Through therapy, coaching, and leadership courses, I can now own all of what makes me who I am today without fear, judgement, pity, shame, or pretending it doesn't exist. Growing up, my invisible disability made me feel like I wasn't enough. I never want anyone to feel that way. I'll never outgrow my dyslexia, but I have moved beyond feeling like I wasn't enough, and I now choose to be relentlessly resilient.

According to *Webster's Dictionary*, resilience is defined as "the ability to recover quickly from difficulties, toughness, and the agility to spring back into shape like elasticity." I didn't bounce back quickly, but I have chosen to bounce back daily. By committing to myself each day that I could get through any challenge—even a disability—I developed a strength that helps me overcome numerous obstacles.

Have you ever felt like the walls are closing in, or like every time you get up you fall back down, or your light has dimmed, that pessimism is dominating your self-talk, or you feel stuck? Do you question why this dark cloud is hovering over you, making you feel lost? You can retrain your brain to be resilient and manifest the life you want, even when you hit an objection or encounter an obstacle. You are not a quitter. You gain strength through struggle, and it's time to dig deep and ignite the light within to guide your next steps.

Following the light within, the fire that ignites your passion, will lead you to joy, and it is your joy that will encourage you to be resilient. Joy is what has led me to dedicating tremendous amounts of time and energy into publishing books on the topics of Growth, Resilience, Intention, and Tenacity, spotlighting women who have G.R.I.T., and developing a G.R.I.T. Community. Keep in mind, even the things in life that bring you joy can require resilience. Creating these books and community brings me joy, but I've also faced many obstacles while creating them. Gathering more than 120 women to author chapters in G.R.I.T. took resilience.

As children, we aren't born with the ability to run. We learn by crawling, falling, walking, falling again, and getting up to try again. Even the seemingly smallest step or army crawl is progress, and a victory. Life will deal us setbacks and defeating experiences, but these struggles are opportunities to push through dark and painful times and emerge through sheer resilience. Lean on your resilience to get through tough times, and your battles will teach you more about who you are. Each obstacle learned might help define your *why*.

Why am I here? I want people to live their best life and I choose to be the person who I needed during my darkest times. Life isn't a fairy tale. At times it can feel like a horror film. We write the manuscript of our lives. The *Deconstructing G.R.I.T. Collection* shares my vision for women's empowerment to bring inspiration to those who are struggling. One of my favorite mottos is: "Say a little; do a lot." This is the way I lead, by teaching G.R.I.T. and creating an inclusive community of women to empower others through storytelling.

We all have negative self-talk trapped in our heads, so be mindful of the power you hold when you hear these defeating thoughts. As they creep into your mind, try to feed your brain with the things it needs during these dark times so you take each step with confidence. Positive words, affirmations, and "I can" statements will blow up that negative energy, but only you will know what you need during these times. Listen to your soul and feed it what it needs to be resilient.

I have had to rely on my utter resilience, and fight tirelessly through fear, heartache, self-doubt, failures, and anxiety. During these times I have questioned my value, my purpose, and I have wondered what I did to bring these hardships into my life. When defeating thoughts seeped in and numbed my future steps, I have felt impaired for my next battles. At times my resilience has pulled me up from my bootstraps, helping me to dust off and keep going. At other times, my resilience has required me to slow down and reevaluate alternatives.

Resilience is a choice. It is a choice to treat failures as experiences. It is a choice to put excuses aside, commit, be persistent, and lead with purpose. What is your Resilience Strategy?

I challenge you to write out your personalized resilience process.

For example: Implementing daily habits; setting three to four long-term goals to achieve within a year; creating an action plan; reading, learning, and listening to topics that aid your growth. Your Resilience Strategy will be your road map to help you during difficult times. Yet it takes daily commitment, persistence, and knowing your purpose.

So what does your custom Resilience Strategy look like? What support, resources, or steps do you need to identify to face the days ahead if confronted with unseen challenges? How will you remain persistent? What is your purpose? What are your habits? Everybody will encounter setbacks. My hope is that by thinking through the tools, you will feel more prepared.

Jennifer Bardot, MA, MS, is a publisher of the *Deconstructing GRIT Collection* and *Owning Your G.R.I.T.*—both international bestselling anthology books available at Target and Walmart. She is featured on the cover of *St. Louis Small Business Monthly* as 2021's Top 100 Person to Know to Help Grow your business and was awarded the President's Circle by Enterprise Bank & Trust. Founder of the GRIT Community—a free women's leadership group—Jennifer holds certificates in the Dare to Lead Training by Brené Brown, Women in Leadership Class of '72, and Leadership St. Louis by Focus St. Louis. She serves at ITEN Lindenwood University, St. Louis University, Washington University, and Fontbonne University. Jennifer is passionate about supporting business owners and female leaders, and is a dedicated mother, community connector, and outdoor adrenaline adventurer.

Roberta Moore

Challenge, Control, and Commitment

Familial bonds are important to those of us who have a human brain, which is partly why I chose to become a Licensed Marriage & Family Therapist. Our families are supposed to help us feel safe, protected, and confident. What does a person do when they realize that their own family does not provide this for them? How can they move forward in life without staying part of the family circle? This was the question I asked myself when my mother died, and the drama that ensued built to a roiling crescendo.

To be sure, there were problems I experienced growing up that set the stage for this monumental event in my life. My mother had an undiagnosed mental health disorder. Left untreated, it ruled my out-of-control family life. Toward me, my mother was cold and emotionally detached. My father, when he was able to be emotionally present, was a more nurturing lifeline. When I lost him to early onset dementia and then death, family relationships that were already strained turned quite bleak. When one of my sisters committed suicide, I felt as if my mother blamed me.

The last time I ever saw this sister, we had an argument about the way her ex-husband was filing a petition to change his name to that of my deceased father's name. I was very scared and believed that was wrong. I begged my sister (who still had a relationship with him) to dissuade him from doing this. She was angry and refused. My mother and other sister witnessed this argument. They both felt I was being unfair to my other sister. This became a pivotal moment in our family history: it caused my mother to remove me from her will and leave most of her property and personal effects to the sister who was caring for her. In addition, I was no longer named as the executrix.

I did not know about this decision until my mother died, when I received a letter from her lawyer. This news came as quite a shock. Not because I wanted new furniture, but because I believe my mother showed her love through giving gifts. It stung like a sharp slap in the face. To me, this meant she thought I was not worthy or lovable enough to divide her assets evenly. It also hurt that my other sister knew about this decision before my mother's death and did not tell me. At the same time, I lost connection with my niece and nephews. When they removed me from their Facebook accounts, I felt like an instant orphan.

At the time this happened, I was building and developing the executive coaching side of my business. To say this event was a setback is to understate its impact on me. I was triggered and had negative thoughts. Everywhere I went, I felt as though I had a big stamp on my forehead that read, "This person is so shameful, her own family disowned her." Although it was difficult to get out of bed every morning and put one foot in front of the other, I continued to work every day. Work gave me a sense of structure and a feeling of security. Work has always been a vehicle for my personal growth, and at this time in my life work continued to be a lifeline of sorts.

Resilience (as defined by the American Psychological Association) is the process and outcome of successfully adapting to challenging life experiences, especially through mental, emotional, or behavioral flexibility. I had to change my perspective. My personal use of the emotional intelligence tools I am certified in aided my own healing. One that stands out as especially beneficial is called HRG, or The Hardiness Resilience Gauge. The HRG is a tool that measures how effectively a person copes with stress. It scientifically measures a person's hardiness and resilience levels. Resilience in this sense is defined as a generalized style of functioning that encompasses cognitive (thinking), emotional (feeling), and behavioral (acting) qualities.

Through self-report, the HRG assessment tool measures three qualities that are relevant for predicting how resilient an individual will be. These three qualities (referred to as Challenge, Control, and Commitment) are defined by this model:

Challenge: seeing change and new experiences as exciting opportunities to learn and develop

Control: belief in one's ability to control or influence events and outcomes

Commitment: a tendency to see the world and day-to-day activities as interesting, meaningful, and having purpose

Scoring high in each of these components facilitates a flexible, confident, and passionate approach to life and ensures a strong degree of resiliency when faced with responding to stressful conditions.

Focusing on this model gave me additional meaning and purpose. I started intentionally daydreaming about the concept of Challenge: Who would I become as I worked my way through to the other side of this experience? How could I become curious about the ways in which this experience would help me become a better version of myself? How could I use my creativity to help me build momentum and guide myself to a place where I could help more people?

Because we are all human beings being raised by humans, no one is perfect. No one gets everything right all the time. Even if a person has been raised by parents who are highly emotionally intelligent, they still experience the ups and downs and traumas of life. No one has all their wants and needs met all of the time. Therefore, my faith tells me that suffering must have a meaning and purpose; Perhaps it is to forge our strength through the fire of trials and tribulations.

The HRG model encourages leaders to view change and novelty as exciting and as an opportunity to learn and grow. I want to be someone who embraces challenge for what it is and for where it can take me. I don't want to be someone who lives out of victim consciousness. This strong desire helps me to find the bright spots in this challenging experience, as it leads me to develop a greater level of compassion for myself and others.

When I think of Control, I think about the concept of surrendering what I can't control (outside circumstances and what other people do) and refocusing on what I can control (my own response and how I choose to feel, think, and behave). I believe I can control and influence the desired outcomes in my life because I also have a very high level of optimism. However, for several years after my mother's death, there were many times when I believed the opposite was true. I struggled with having a sense of agency and self-efficacy.

Using this concept, I worked on writing and completing my first book: *Emotional Intelligence: Unleashing the Secret Power of Emotional Intelligence*. The process of reflection, contemplation, and writing helped pull me forward by focusing on my clients' success stories. I wrote about the work we did together to successfully raise their emotional intelligence. Writing the book helped me reconnect to myself as a person and helped me believe in my ability to coach clients to success.

The concept of Commitment is the ability to be fully engaged and present in your life, and to find it rewarding and fulfilling. I am willing to work hard to accomplish my goals. Since I was a little girl, I tried to help everyone in my family be happier, fight less, and get along better. I think those tendencies were born out of my desperation to escape what I experienced as a chaotic and unpredictable family life. To cope with unhappiness, I committed an inordinate amount of time to schoolwork and getting good grades. That was something I could control and doing so made me feel safe.

Today my feeling of Commitment feels as vital as breathing. The daily routine of prayer, meditation, body movement, and affirmations helps me leave victim consciousness just a little bit further behind.

There is a saying that time heals all wounds. I am not so certain. I think if we want to heal our wounds, we must pay attention to the parts of ourselves that got hurt. If we want to be resilient, we must keep the concepts of Challenge, Commitment, and Control in mind and work with them. I would be lying if I told you I was totally healed; but I am certainly better. I think Carl Jung was correct: healing comes along in a circumambulating manner. As we go along, we continually circle back around to the beginning of the problem, yet each time we relive it, we are doing so from a higher level of perspective. When the clouds of negative thoughts part, and I can see the truth, I recognize that every family member did the very best they could do. We were all joined together in a common quest for worthiness.

EQ-i Coach founder, executive coach, and author of *Emotion at Work: Unleashing the Secret Power of Emotional Intelligence* Roberta Moore draws on nearly four decades in executive coaching, professional services, and psychotherapy to help her clients understand and unleash the power of emotional intelligence (EQ) through individual and team EQ coaching, team workshops, and EQ assessments and audits. Moore's work earned her a 2020 Enterprising Women of the Year Award, one of the most prestigious recognitions for women business owners, as well as a 2020 Globee Women World Female Achievers Champion of the Year Award and a 2021 Stevies Award. Moore is also a member of the Forbes Coaches Council and publishes monthly articles in *Forbes*. She is a contributing author to the 2020 book *The Anatomy of Accomplishment: Your Guide to Bigger, Better, Bolder Business Results*, an anthology of professional wisdom from women business leaders across the country.

Emily Pitts

Kindness Respect Resilience

Resilience is as much of a necessity in life as the air we breathe to survive. When the going gets tough, resilience helps us survive through disappointments, rejections, hurt, illness, tragedies, broken hearts, and even death. What we have learned is that it is not what happens to us, but how we handle it. Faith and resilience are what get us through it all.

As I reflect on my life, I know that without resilience I would not be where I am or who I am today. I was raised in Chattanooga, Tennessee, in a middle-class family who encouraged me and made me believe if I trusted in the Lord, treated people with kindness and respect, and worked hard, I could do anything. Three generations of women who were teachers in my family instilled in me the values of being a life learner and a cheerful giver. My two older sisters and older brother supported me and encouraged me every day. But as we all know, even with all the support in the world, one must learn some things for oneself, while being open to learning from others.

After obtaining my undergraduate degree in Atlanta, I pursued a career in sales, as I always believed I would be a good businesswoman. I applied for a job with a pharmaceutical company, but, unfortunately, there were very few African American women in pharmaceutical sales at that time. A drug company hired me into an entry-level position. I was determined to prove myself and to get promoted to sales as soon as possible. The manager was surprised that I wanted to be in pharmaceutical sales. He gave me a big book of medical terminology and told me when I finished reading it to let him know and we could talk about a sales career. I thought, "I wonder, does he think he has discouraged me?" which motivated me even more. You guessed it. When I finished the book and went back to him to claim my role in sales, he instead gave me another book to read and told me, again, to come back when I finished it. It became apparent that this was going nowhere. But I have always believed things happen for a reason.

Disappointed but not defeated, I heard that a financial services firm was recruiting. I had always been interested in finance and investing, so I applied to work in the operations center for this firm and was hired. I gained valuable experience and even more interest in becoming a financial advisor. Remember: sales was my dream. What I did not realize was that there are significant differences between selling tangible goods versus intangible products like stocks, bonds, mutual funds, and more.

Entering the financial services industry as an African American woman provided me many opportunities to learn, for sure. It was a white, male-dominated industry, not accustomed to people of color in equivalent roles. Making a positive difference in the lives of others was the way I was raised and in my DNA. So the financial services industry was a perfect entrée to making a difference in the lives of my people and anybody who was willing to listen to a woman who once was a little Black girl from Chattanooga.

After working in the financial services industry for a couple of years, I was convinced that I wanted to be a financial advisor and help people reach their financial goals to retire, build a nest egg, or put their kids through college. I applied to become a licensed financial advisor.

But, again, African American women financial advisors were few and far between at that time. It's not much better, even today. A firm must sponsor a candidate to take the Series 7 exam to become licensed as a financial advisor. Unfortunately, the writing was on the wall again that I would not get the support I needed from leadership.

So, I left that firm and went to another major financial services firm, where I became the assistant under the operations manager. After a few years, I decided to pursue getting licensed again. Unfortunately, I was informed the company was looking for folks with sales experience and not folks who had spent their careers in the operational aspect of the business. "What now?" I wondered. What will my next move be, after almost three years with this company?

My resilience kicked in stronger than ever. I left and went to another large financial services firm where I hit the jackpot. It was a discount firm that facilitated stock and other trades but did not give financial advice. Everyone had to be licensed to enter the trades, however. I worked at this firm for nine years, until I decided I wanted to advise my clients as a full-service broker. So I stepped out in faith to work for a firm on commission versus the salary I was making at the discount firm.

After a couple of weeks, I realized that the new company's core values did not align with mine. I politely exited without knowing what I would do next.

Here's where the story turns. Throughout my ten-year career in the financial services industry, I had heard about a company named Edward Jones, where every financial advisor is provided with their own branch office and with training and everything needed to be successful, if you are willing to do the work. That sounded too good to be true, but I applied and was hired by this dream company. I was most appreciative of the mentors I gained who believed in me (before I believed myself) that I could finally become a successful financial advisor. Even more of a surprise—most of my mentors were white men. I learned that you never know where your blessings will come from. Sometimes the people who you think will be there for you may not, and the people you think will not, will.

After approximately four years of building my own Edward Jones office and mentoring others, I was invited to become a Limited Partner. This was a life-changing experience, as I became part owner in a major organization. While my part was very small in the grand scheme of things, I was a partner nonetheless. This gave me the confidence and boost to take my business to the next level. It also inspired me even more to share what I had learned and to pay it forward by helping others be successful in the business.

After five years of helping many individuals and families reach their financial goals, I received the surprise of my life: I was invited to become the first African American woman General Partner at Edward Jones. I had never focused on becoming a General Partner because it never occurred to me that I could be one. I was the first General Partner who looked like me, and I am thrilled to say there are several more today. It was resilience that brought me through all the noes, the setbacks, the disappointments, and gave me the ability to get back up and keep pushing forward to what God had in store for me. If we stay true to ourselves, and in all that we do try to leave people in a better place than when they met them, our blessings will come when we least expect them. I was blessed to retire after twenty-five wonderful years with Edward Jones as a financial advisor and an executive leading diversity and inclusion.

I thought I would enjoy retirement with my amazing husband and do a little consulting, but my story continues. I was invited to join the leadership of the highly respected Lindenwood University in St. Charles, Missouri. This role uses all my life and professional experiences to make a difference in the lives of faculty, staff, and the students, who are the reason why we are there. This is how resilience has impacted my life, and I highly recommend it to anyone who has dreams.

Now let me share a few pieces of advice that will enable and magnify your resilience:

- Remain humble and grateful for what you have. If you aren't thankful for what you have, why should God bless you with more?

- Give credit where credit is due. Be a blessing to someone else by shining a light on them. Your time will come.

- Be a life learner. Only if you continue to learn will you remain relevant.

- Never let someone else define your capabilities. No one knows you better than you.

- Don't hold grudges. Holding negative energy inside takes away your readiness for the blessings God has in store for you.

- Pay it forward. We are all standing on the shoulders of others. Don't forget to let someone stand on yours.

- Be a cheerful giver. To whom much is given, much is required.

Emily Pitts brings more than thirty-five years of corporate experience developing and influencing leadership teams at all levels, and she has a deep understanding and passion for ensuring organizations achieve business objectives while maintaining an inclusive approach.

Emily became the first African American woman General Partner at Edward Jones. During her twenty-five-year career she served as a Financial Advisor helping clients reach their financial goals, and prior to retirement was the General Partner responsible for Inclusion & Diversity.

She currently serves as the Chief Diversity Officer and Director of the Center for Diversity at Lindenwood University.

Emily has received numerous local and national awards and is often sought after as a keynote speaker. She serves on the boards of the Boys and Girls Club of Greater St. Louis, St. Louis Urban League, YMCA, and the St. Louis Alzheimer's Association. Emily is also a member of the Executive Leadership Council and Chief organization.

Michelle Fitter

Hard to Love

Everyone experiences different things in their childhood that contribute to the person they become.

As the eldest of three, I took care of my siblings while my mom spent many evenings at the bars or brought the party home. She eventually married, but there was still a lot of dysfunction in our lives. Each of my siblings has chosen a separate path in life.

While most young children are excited to go to the store with their mom because they may get a cool new toy, I was always nervous because I knew it was wrong. Many of these trips ended with an officer escorting her out of the store. I was with her multiple times when she was caught shoplifting. It became apparent that this was a sickness, not a money issue.

The pivotal incident happened one evening, as the sun was going down. I was sitting on the front porch of our house, which sat up on a hill. I watched as a caravan of law enforcement came up the long country road. Immediately, my heart sank, as I knew where they were headed. I ran inside and shook my mom from her normal afternoon nap. She jumped from the bed, gathered a suitcase full of items, and told me to "get rid of it." I grabbed the suitcase and my siblings and dashed out the door. Running through the yards between houses, I tried to dispose of the suitcase, but law enforcement surrounded the house and retrieved it.

Then they tore our house apart. They removed large trash bags of marijuana and other illegal substances, firearms, and any items of value that were assumed to have been purchased with illegal funds. My mom was arrested. My siblings and I stayed at the neighbor's house until our grandparents picked us up. The next day the raid was all over the local news.

From that day forward, my family fell apart. I changed schools from a rural Catholic high school to a magnet school in the city. I met some lifelong, supportive friends, but life was different. I knew that I didn't want to be that person who used my upbringing as an excuse for failure or to repeat the cycle.

After the raid, my mom was in and out of jail. I stayed with my grandparents, who were truly my saviors and lifeline. Out of spite, she had me removed from my grandparents' home and placed in a foster home on Christmas day. As I sat in a stranger's home for the holidays, I began to learn what resilience was. Still a child, I was thrown into the world, bitter and lost, but I realized I had to make choices and act.

I went to college in Kansas City and became sick after my first semester due to the family stresses. I came home and got a full-time job and went to school part-time.

During the next few years, I relentlessly tried to be the "fixer." My mom was sentenced to five years in prison on my birthday. Despite everything, I visited often, and I took my siblings in and tried to help my family get along. Unfortunately, that wasn't possible. I drove fast cars and partied a lot. I had relationships where I treated the good ones badly and the bad ones good.

Then I met my husband, Jeff, when I was twenty-two years old. We were both reeling from similar family situations. Our struggles and determination grew into a strong, loving bond, and we vowed to build a quality life together. We worked hard through multiple jobs at a time, while attending college classes and having two baby girls, Brittni and Ciarra Jamie (CJ).

I completed an associate's degree and continued to go to night school for Accounting Information Systems Management. At the same time, Jeff traveled for work and the kids were getting into sports and activities. I never completed that degree, but I learned a lot that I'm now using in the business world today.

As Jeff and I were promoted in our respective roles, our income also grew. My family's perception shifted from me being the "fixer" to being "better than" them. This was difficult for me and caused me to put up a shell around my heart. Ultimately, this made me hard to love as I sheltered myself from most relationships and didn't open myself to many people.

I advanced in my role as an account manager and was promoted to an account executive. This was a demanding position, while at the same time my girls were both playing sports, nearing high school graduation, and looking for colleges while Jeff was traveling even more with his job. This was a challenging time for Mama. As our girls grew up and became more independent, I wondered, "What will I do when they leave?"

I was losing sleep and questioning what the next phase of my life would be. I needed to get some relief and find some direction. I took a short leave of absence to clear my head. When I returned to work, the same boss who had previously given me praises and bonuses treated me poorly. I chose to put my phone and badge on the HR manager's desk and never looked back. I literally walked out on a $100,000 job.

In the months after my resignation, I stayed home and spent time with my kids. I determined that a job does not define who you are and it's imperative to be confident in your abilities. Soon after, I took a position at another firm as an account executive. After four years, I made a professional move to MMA, where I have excelled. I am currently VP, Senior Account Executive,

Client Strategy Manager, where I strategize with my staff of account executives to bring solutions to our Employee Benefits clients.

In 2017, after a turn of events in Jeff's job, we purchased Super Smokers BBQ. Jeff is "living the dream," as he would say, as he's not working a corporate job and getting on an airplane every week. The first two years were a lot of work to rebuild a dying brand. The key was connecting with the community and delivering a quality product.

In 2020, the pandemic hit, and the world turned upside down. Restaurants were closed and uncertainty surrounded our dreams. Once again in our life, we were forced to determine how to survive. We held it together as a family and remained strong through adversity. We got creative with neighborhood food truck events, feeding first responders, and curbside service. With the support of the community (and some relief funds), we survived the worst of 2020.

In June of 2021, we opened our second location and expanded the menu to include Cajun cuisine. If we weren't crazy enough, in September of 2022 we purchased Case and Bucks, a bar and grill located in Barnhart, Missouri. Our family manages three restaurants and three food trucks.

Restaurant life is hard, but every day we get up and try to figure out how to be better. Both daughters play important roles in our day-to-day operations. Learning how to keep family and work separate has been a difficult task, but my kids are *amazing*! We have accomplished so much together.

Jeff and I have been married for twenty-eight years. The girls are all grown up and married now. Our sons-in-law, Brandon and Nick, have joined the family, and we couldn't be more appreciative of the lives they are building with our girls. Our two grandbabies, Elliott Rayne and Taytum Jamie, have solidified that all our work is worth it. Everything we do every day is for the family we have built, and we continue to make lasting memories.

Bringing life full circle, after the loss of her home and a serious medical diagnosis, my mom moved in with us three years ago. I try every day to leave the past in the past and take care of her. But my heart is truly damaged. Now I am struggling with having to let go and move her to a facility where they can take better care of her. One would think it would feel like retribution, but instead I feel guilt and sadness.

My family and friends have been helpful and supportive, and I am so grateful. My husband is my rock (and roll). We have had our ups and downs, but neither of us would be where we are without the other. Having my mom in our home has been extra challenging. Shout out to Jeff Fitter!

Resilience can be a lonely choice. I have had to set some tough boundaries. But difficult roads often lead to beautiful destinations, and I have a beautiful life!

Michelle Fitter is an author in *Resilience* and Title Sponsor (Super Smokers BBQ + CAJUN).

Michelle is Vice President, Client Strategy Manager at Marsh & McLennan Agency (MMA), a Fortune 500 company and professional services firm in risk, strategy, and people. Michelle is co-owner of Super Smokers BBQ and Case & Bucks restaurants and food trucks.

She earned her Associates of Business Administration in 1999 and studied Accounting Information Systems.

Michelle has over thirty years of experience in the health insurance industry working in claims, service, and implementation. Michelle's current role is to consult with large group accounts including Public Entity and Academic Institutions. She also leads a team of account executives who bring strategic solutions to their clients.

Her focus in the restaurants is financial planning, accounting, and strategic operations.

Michelle has a crafting business with her daughters and enjoys spending time at the lake with her family.

Aloha Kelly

The Gray Area

I could tell you a story that shows how I became successful after many hardships in my life. I could say that without the dark times I wouldn't be who I am today. I could pretend that all those horrible things I had to endure have somehow made my life better. Although there may be some truth in all this, I am still unable to cope with what has happened to me. Instead, I have pushed these things deeper and deeper until they don't "exist" anymore, and I fill the emptiness with as much light as possible.

You cannot have light without dark.

As a photographer, I have learned that to create an image that has impact, light and dark aspects need to be properly and delicately in balance. Without light there is no darkness. The contrast between the light and the dark has many tones in between, so although there is no light without darkness, there are also layers upon layers of gray area.

It is within this gray area that resilience is found.

When I am faced with a difficult life situation, I can hear my mother's voice in my head: "Just pick yourself up by the bootstraps and keep moving." Even when I was a small child and faced with a hard task, she would say those exact words to me. At seventeen years old, I moved out of my parents' house. I was determined to keep moving even though adulthood hit me harder than I thought it would. I was barely out of high school, living on my own with my soon-to-be husband and managing things day by day. I had to figure out how to pay for college because my parents couldn't. I worked multiple jobs and kept my head down. At nineteen, freshly married and the whole world ahead of us, 9/11 happened. War happened—a war that completely changed the course of my life over-night. Not only did my brother join the military, but my husband decided he needed to fight too.

The morning he left for bootcamp, I tried to be strong. Instead, my best friend found me huddled up in my car in the driveway, after four hours of crying and panic attacks that drove me into a depression that would affect me for many years. Of course, there was my mom's voice in my head . . . just pick yourself up and keep moving forward. So I did. I made it through bootcamp, Advanced Individual Training (AIT), and a move to Texas. After his first deployment, we became parents. During the second deployment, we divorced. We had built a life together, half of which my husband wasn't even present for. I lost my home, my extended family, and my support system . . . all from war.

After the divorce, I created a second chance for myself. I went back to college, enrolled my child in the Head Start program, moved back in with my parents temporarily, and tried to just keep my gaze toward the future. Soon after I found an apartment. My ex-husband dropped a custody battle in my lap. I was a single mother, working minimum wage at two different jobs and attending school full time—but that wasn't enough. I borrowed money from my parents to pay lawyers, and at times chose between paying them or paying rent, paying utilities, or buying food. Eventually, I got kicked out and moved in with someone I had barely started dating because I had nowhere else to go.

Things were great for a short time, even with the co-parenting chaos. My child was diagnosed with ADHD, and because the school couldn't handle it, we had to switch schools mid-year, forcing us to move into a different district and uproot our home once again. Although this move was a bit more stable for the kids, it was not for me, either emotionally or physically. I discovered that the man I was living with was a heroin addict and couldn't control it. With no health insurance, we sought simple treatment options, and eventually there was some improvement. I would never consider the decision to marry him a mistake, because the love I had for him was stronger than the love he had for himself. Seeing him regain some control over his addiction was amazing. I hoped we could continue to a place where he'd stay clean. He was functioning normally, working, and seemed to be exceeding expectations. I was still working full time *and* running my photography business, shooting weddings on the weekends. All seemed to be right in the world for the first time in a long time.

In April of 2015, I decided to take a big risk and leave the stability of a nine-to-five job and become a full-time business owner amid managing my husband's addiction. I was finally doing what I loved, our kids were doing well in school, we had routines down, we bought a home, and were no longer living paycheck to paycheck. It was a good time for me to start this new journey into entrepreneurship.

My mother-in-law decided it was a good idea to send my husband away for a specialized treatment that would potentially keep him clean. If you know anything about recovery, you know that it's much more than a quick physical fix. The mental aspect needs to be dealt with too—and this treatment did not do both. When he returned, physically clean from the drugs, I saw real hope and life in his eyes. I felt like maybe, just maybe, we'd have a chance to build what we had dreamed of all these years. I encouraged him to attend AA meetings and find a psychiatrist, but that wasn't well received. We fought about whether the treatment was worth it, though ultimately it was a step in the right direction. Unfortunately, this part of my story ends rather abruptly. Four months after the treatment, my husband relapsed and died from an overdose.

The moments that followed news of his death are blurry. Even now, seven years later, I cannot explain what it feels like to be a widow. Those feelings are replayed over and over in my head like a broken record, and I can't seem to get away from the darkness. It's otherworldly; it makes you see yourself from another dimension, like you're trapped inside a cage deep in the ocean without a chance of rescue. I wouldn't wish this on my worst enemy. It's terrifying to feel helpless and lost in a sea of unrecognized emotions. To drown in waves that don't stop . . . What do you do?

You listen.

You listen for the inner voice. The one that keeps telling you to "pick yourself up by the bootstraps and keep moving." And so you do. You move forward. You hold your head high and search for the light. Even in the darkest depths of the ocean, you can still find light. You just have to keep swimming.

I find myself once again in the gray area between darkness and light. This is when resilience kicks in.

After my husband's passing, I realized I had quite a mess to clean up. Of course, I avoided as much as possible and instead threw myself headfirst into my business. I took what was left of the darkness and used it as fuel—like coal to a fire—and created the stepping stones to my empire. It took many years to rebuild what I had lost, and I had a lot of help along the way. I was blessed to find a man who not only protects what is left of my heart but allows me to continue to grieve. He has supported me immensely in a way I can never repay. With his love and devotion adding fuel to my fire, I have created a life I never dreamed I could have. For that, I am forever grateful.

I have concluded that darkness is necessary for there to be light. It's not the other way around. It's not even something you can create. Darkness has to happen, most of the time completely out of your control, in order to force you to find the light. The gray area in between is where you fight, where you struggle, where you give up, and where you try again. I promise that the light is there. Pick yourself up by the bootstraps and keep going, even when you think you can't. It's going to be tough, but it's not forever. Resilience can be found. Look for it in the gray area.

Aloha is the owner and lead photographer of Aloha Kelly Photography and Love Exposed Boudoir. She is an award-winning and published photographer specializing in Intimate and Empowering Women's Portraiture. Her goal is to show women a side of themselves they don't see every day and support them through their self-love discoveries. Through her photography business, Aloha teaches women to be strong, motivated, and unapologetically themselves.

Aloha was born and raised in St. Louis, Missouri, where she currently resides with her husband, child, and four cats. Aloha enjoys yoga, a Starbucks drink in the morning, and obsessing over anything pink. If you can't find her in the Midwest, she's probably on a beach somewhere soaking up the sunshine. Aloha has been a photographer for more than fifteen years and continues to work with clients regularly in her studio in addition to helping creative female entrepreneurs fulfill their business dreams and goals.

Jennifer Church

Can't Never Could

We all know whose mother said, "Life is like a box of chocolates; you never know what you're going to get." Well, my mother had her own saying. She would tell us, "Can't never could!" Then she would always add, "Don't tell me what you can't do; tell me what you can do." This is where my resilience was born and cultivated. Thanks, Mom.

I have learned that resilience comes from within you. It is the ability to bounce back from difficult situations. To face the mountain ahead of you and enjoy the climb. To learn new tips and a few tricks along the way, and to pull from the ones you have already learned in order to overcome and succeed. Resilience is the ability to stay motivated and realistic in the journey to fill yourself with confidence and purpose.

The worst part of resilience is that it usually comes from being uncomfortable, or that a difficult situation has come along and taken away the "normal" path you were on. True resilience is usually found during the darkest parts of your life. When these things happen, hopefully you will dig deep within yourself and find your resilience, your fight, your drive, and your motivation to keep going, to keep pushing, to climb the hill. These will help you get back to your normal, or better yet help you grow. You have to enter the darkness to find your light. You will bounce back and most of the time come out better in the end, stronger than you knew you could be, with more confidence, flexibility, and optimism.

There are several key ingredients in making the *Resilience Stew*. Realism, flexibility, purpose, confidence, inner work, optimism, and persistence. Here's what your recipe looks like:

- Be *realistic* to accept the way things really are, to understand the actual situation and wrap your mind around it so you have a level head when thinking of your solution to deal with the situation.

- Learn to be *flexible* and adaptable so you can go with the flow and ride even the roughest wave. You know the calm is coming eventually and that you will overcome the troubled waters. If you can manage to go with the flow, you will have not only control over the response to the situation but control of yourself.

- Have a *purpose* for doing things. Find a sense of meaning that gives you motivation and strength to keep going, keep trying, and moving forward.

- Be *confident* knowing that in the end you will rise above and conquer no matter how difficult the problem may seem. This is the ability to believe in yourself. Do not let loss define you; only give it the power to motivate you.

- Know how to do the *inner work*. There are many times your inner voice holds you back. What you tell yourself is usually much worse than anything anyone has ever said to you. You must repair the damage, understand your weaknesses, fill the holes in your soul, plant the seeds of love in your heart, and get rid of the negative thoughts in your brain. Thrive—do not just survive. Life is not a destination, it is journey. You're not here merely to survive but to live a life worth living.

- Make *optimism* a core value. Know that your cup is always half full and will soon be overflowing with all the great things you are filling it with.

- Be *persistent*. It pays off. It's not all figured out if you do it once; rather it gets worked out by continuing to do it over and over again while learning along the way.

Each of us has had disappointments, adversity, or just plain terrible things happen in our lives. Things that we wish we could make go away or things that we wish never happened. But making a wish does not work very often. Cultivate your inner core and your resilience.

In 1998 I was blessed with the most precious baby girl ever born! She was beautiful and perfect in every way. I was twenty-six years old, a single mother, broke and scared. I had no idea what I was doing, and there was no manual to refer to for help. I tried, I succeeded a lot, and I failed at times too. Overall, I would call it a win because it was my purpose; I knew above anything else my most important role was being a mother, the best one I could be. Morgan, my daughter, is my lifelong purpose. Above all else, I am so blessed she is mine.

I work with the largest equipment rental company in the world, United Rentals. I started as an outside sales rep and currently I am a Strategic Account Manager. I manage a handful of high-revenue accounts and act as a single point of contact for them across the country. When I started in this role in 2003, I was one of three females in the entire St. Louis area in equipment rental. Construction—wow! As a woman working hands-on in the field, it was a tough industry to walk into, or rather scratch, claw, and hang on to for dear life. It was unforgiving, but I knew I could handle whatever came my way. I dug in my resilience bucket and pulled out my persistence. I told myself every day, "Keep showing up, you will figure it out." Thankfully, twenty years later, I am still here. I have been a part of building St. Louis and have seen some amazing construction feats. I wear my boots and hard hat with pride; I have earned every scratch on them.

Knowing that relationships were the key to my success in this industry, I quickly joined several organizations. The American Subcontractors Association–Midwest Council holds my heart. I made numerous relationships within this organization, and the people became part of my extended family. After a few years as a member and serving as chairperson for a few of their committees, I was asked to sit on the board of directors. I gratefully accepted. It was not long before I was elected as one of the chairs, and in my third year I became the president of the ASA-MWC. What an honor! I am one of only three female presidents to have served so far for the MWC. This was met with some opposition at first, but I pulled out that realistic resilience and lead with confidence and purpose, knowing there was a job to do and that changes needed to be made for the betterment of the members and what we had to offer them. Two things I am most proud of during my one-year term: making safety our main priority focus, and creating a women in construction group, the ASA Women's Council–She's Built For This. Currently, I sit on the board of directors for the National American Subcontractors Association. I was humbled by this invitation and again will use realistic resilience to know what needs to be done and why, to face the challenges, and to press on with making a difference.

In 2006, I was diagnosed with rheumatoid arthritis. The arthritis community calls us *warriors*, which is true in every definition of that word. My disease has taught me so many valuable lessons on how to see things in life from more than one viewpoint. It's also taught me a hundred different ways to try to open a jar on those days that your hands don't work! Resilience in the form of flexibility: some days are good, some are bad. All days are doable.

In 2017, I fell into another dark hole, this time in the form of a brain tumor. Don't worry, it is hanging out in my meninges and isn't really causing a problem yet. But once again, resilience showed up in the best way—through optimism. A brain tumor isn't going to stop me or slow me down; after all, it could be worse.

There are many other times in my life that I have needed resilience. I am thankful that I have learned to pull from my bag of tricks and find whatever is needed to keep pushing on. The future is unknown for all of us, and this in itself brings out resilience. This time it takes shape in the form of confidence. Be confident in the things you do. Do them with intent and purpose. Take advice from others, learn from experience, think about things rationally, know the reality, and do your best. Don't forget it's OK to ask for help when you need it.

I urge you to always find your resilience. Do the inner work and know where you are strong and where the weaknesses are. The weak areas are the ones you need to cultivate, grow, and understand. Know that everything will be fine in the long run. Consider this an investment in yourself; you will be prepared no matter what lies ahead. So whether you tell yourself you can or tell yourself you can't, either way you are right! Create your own Resilience Recipe dish and serve it up!

Jennifer currently resides in St. Louis, Missouri, where she was born and raised. Morgan, her daughter, is her greatest love. Jennifer is in the role of Strategic Account Manager with United Rentals, a Fortune 500 company that she has called home for twenty years. She is a past president of The American Subcontractors Association–Midwest Council. She currently sits on the National Board of Directors for the American Subcontractors and is an internationally bestselling author. Her favorite hobbies include family, golf, boating, and art.

Gabriela Ramirez

More Than 26.2 Miles

A month before the Chicago Marathon, my daughter Marcela passed away.

The day it happened, my daughter Adriana called me as I was driving to a meeting. I don't remember what she said or how it was that she told me, but I knew it was bad. I remember suddenly telling her, "I am lost," because at that moment I couldn't figure out where I was. All I could think about was getting to her house, but I had no idea how to do that. She said, "Calm down, pull to the side of the road, and tell me what street you are on." My eyes filled with tears. The only thing I could think was, "My daughter is guiding me. I'm supposed to be the mother. I'm supposed to be protecting my children." But I couldn't. I didn't. My world fell apart.

I finally found my way to Adriana's house, and we hugged and cried in disbelief. Early that morning, our Doll, her childhood nickname, had overdosed in her Michigan apartment. We slowly started to call our family, beginning with my sister Marcela, then my nephew. We knew these were going to be difficult conversations. The calls got harder as the reality of what happened started to set in, and how our lives were changed forever.

Early the next morning, we drove to Michigan. Adriana and my sisters went to Doll's apartment and made the arrangements. My thoughts ran in a loop: "It's not happening! This isn't real." But it was, and the only thing I could do with myself while they were at the apartment was to go for a run.

I was training for the Chicago Marathon, which was coming up soon. As I ran, I cried and yelled, enjoying the physical pain as I ran those miles. Over the weekend, as her friends in Michigan started to get the news, and more and more people reached out, the weight and reality of the situation overwhelmed me. Accepting condolences was not easy, and I was frustrated by spending time consoling and reassuring some callers. "Is this normal," I wondered, "that I am having to be the stronger person when it's my child who's no longer with us?"

So, I ran every morning—to release my stress, train my body, be by myself, and to just cry. When people learned I was still training, they were surprised. "You can run next year," they said. But I couldn't stop. Only the physical exertion of the run made the pain in my heart bearable. Only then could I be mad at the world without judgement, or pity. I kept running and training. When I ran the Chicago Marathon barely one month later, I knew my daughter was with me. My mind played tricks on me, as I would look up and see her in the crowd, or someone who looked like her. But I felt her presence anyway. The joy of running the marathon and the physical exertion, if only for six hours and thirty-four minutes, relieved the pain in my heart and the loss and emptiness I had been feeling since the day we got the news.

Along the way, amazing people helped keep me in the game of life by supporting me in one way or another. This is where I found resilience. The power in getting up every day. In going out to run every day despite the blisters and the gaping hole in my heart. Training for the marathon helped me learn to respond to the stress of the run, and it became the tool to help me overcome the pain and heartache of losing my child. This difficult loss, the loss of my son the previous year, and other painful times in my life have caused me to do a lot of introspective thinking. I have learned a lot, and I invite you to think about how we can support each other and how we *receive* that support.

Open up and accept the embrace.

Share when you are asked how you are.

Accept the invitation to be vulnerable.

Ask for help.

It will be so much more beneficial for you and others in your life.

I have learned to be kind to myself. I have learned to quiet that inner critic that often has me believing I must go through difficult times by myself, or, worse yet, that I somehow deserve them. I did a lot of soul-searching during all those miles that led me to the Chicago Marathon. The miles meant more than just the physical exertion, the pain and blisters; they were my way out of the heartache. The training was not just for the marathon; it was a way to keep going, to keep my sanity, and to build the resilience that my lungs needed, my body required, and my mind and heart welcomed to get through that painful month. I found meaning in my life and a sense of purpose in those runs and preparations. I rediscovered that being resilient means facing sorrow and sadness and not turning away from it.

On the morning of October 10, one month after my Doll's death, I arrived in Chicago. I wasn't sure if I could run 26.2 miles because I was so sad and mad at God and the world all at the same time. But all the training leading up to the marathon gave me purpose and helped my heart heal. All those miles gave me something to focus on other than the pain and the gaping hole in my life. I also don't know where I would be without my family and friends, who for those first thirty days did not let me be by myself. They checked on me before and after every run. Even if I was working, they were in touch with me. And, if I'd let them, my mom and sister would have gone to work with me! I am so glad I let them in and quit trying to face my pain and grief alone.

Shortly after starting to put pen to paper for this chapter, I found comfort in this quote from Ernest Hemingway: "The world breaks everyone and afterward many are strong in the broken places."

Read this quote whenever you need to be reminded to keep moving, keep trying, and keep sharing your story and your lessons learned. Our voices are a source of resilience, and we are strengthened by each other's experiences as we learn from each other and rebound from difficult things.

Originally from Guanajuato, Mexico, and inspired by her own experience growing up an immigrant in the United States, Gabriela Ramirez-Arellano has a passion and commitment to help others.

Gabriela found her voice advocating for and helping small business owners achieve their dreams through her work at CORTEX and through her podcasts, *Auténtico* and *We Live Here Auténtico* in collaboration with St. Louis Public Radio. Her work at the BALSA Foundation promotes social equity and prosperity.

An author and marathon runner, a Mizzou (University of Missouri–Columbia) and Lindenwood University graduate, Gabriela and her husband own Don Emilianos in O'Fallon, Missouri, and recently celebrated their seven-year anniversary. Just recently, Gabriela crossed off a bucket list item by competing in a local *Dancing with the Stars* competition to raise money for human trafficking. She is most proud of raising amazing children who inspire her to help make the world a better place regardless of the obstacles and resistance.

Julie Lawson

Get Up

I lay on my back and stared at the sun as it struggled to make its way from behind the clouds. Every inch of me hurt, so I remained still. My mind searched for understanding; I wanted desperately to know why I was here. Not in the literal sense—I was here because I had just been the victim of a violent assault. But why me? Why now? What had I done (or not done) in my life that led to this moment?

I shifted my legs. They felt like boulders beneath me, and I gave into their weight. I looked again to the sky and asked God for help. A dark, menacing cloud rolled in front of the sun in response, and the twilight air around me grew cold and damp. *Even God can't look at me right now*, I thought.

My soul winced, so I forced my thoughts from the existential to the practical. I needed to get out of there. To get help, to figure out what was next. I tried to stand. I couldn't move. I tried again and failed. Panic started to set in: What if I can't get up? Who will find me? Is this all there will be to my life? My breath quickened.

"Get up," I heard faintly in the back of my mind.

I can't, I thought. *My legs aren't working and …*

"Get up." The voice was stronger this time.

I pushed back. "It hurts," I said aloud.

"Get up!" it insisted.

My mind raced. I was in full panic mode, unsure of how I would get to my car, to medical help, to home … or how I would navigate a life forever altered. I was dizzy from trauma and uncertainty, and I wanted to give in to it.

"All you have to do is *get up*," it said, more gently this time.

I was suddenly curious about this stranger in my mind. It sounded like my voice, but these weren't my words. Carefully, and with great effort, I got up. I took one step, then another. And a few more. Soon I was walking steadily toward healing.

That day I first heard the voice of an indomitable spirit: resilience.

On a bright May morning I lay still in bed, watching the ceiling fan *thump, thump, thump*. I listened to birds chirping happily outside and wondered if they could infect me with their optimism. This was my second day in bed, though I wasn't sick. My mind searched for understanding: What had just happened? Why didn't it work out? What had I done (or not done) to bring me to this point?

Two days before, I had walked out of a toxic relationship. The man I had given three years of my life to had become verbally and emotionally abusive, then unfaithful. When he'd been caught in his lies, his behavior on the way out was particularly brutal. Rejection, betrayal, and uncertainty vied for the top position in my heart. I felt like I couldn't breathe under the weight of disappointment and heartache. I had no idea how to move forward, how to remedy the sadness I felt. I had built my life around him. I had trusted him. I believed his unthinkable message: that I deserved his cruel behavior. How could I heal from that? Would I ever find love again? What was I going to do now?

"Get up," I heard.

Hey, I know you! It's been a while, I thought.

"Just get up. You'll figure out the rest later."

"I can't," I argued. "I'm too heartbroken ..."

"*Get up*," the voice urged. "He doesn't get to keep you down."

I sighed, then stood from the bed. I showered and ate. Before I knew it, one step at a time, I was walking toward healing.

Several years later I lay on a small table staring up at a single bright bulb. My throat hurt, and I was told to remain still. I wondered why I was here. Why me? Why now? I whispered a prayer under my breath as the oncologist abruptly clicked off the light.

"OK, Julie, I'll look at the biopsy results when they come back from the lab and will contact you. It'll be a few days."

My mind reeled. I had struggled with Hashimoto's disease for years, but this was my first brush with cancer. I was paralyzed with fear.

"Get up," I heard from the back of my mind.

Not you again, I thought. This voice had become too familiar. I heard it when I struggled to find purpose after quitting a terrible job. After loved ones had passed and I wasn't sure how to overcome my grief. After so many of life's trials, big and small. It was the same dull, seemingly useless message echoing in my mind when what I needed most was brilliant advice or loving encouragement. It was beginning to irritate me.

"Get up," it said again. "You just have to get up. Get dressed."

Not wanting to argue with myself, I stood. I went through the motions, composing myself and finding my way to the waiting area.

"How was it?" my husband asked lovingly. I was required to have a driver with me for the procedure, but I was so glad he was here for emotional support. "I got up, so that's something." I laughed. He grabbed my hand, and I took the first step toward healing. (I'm glad to say that I'm healthy today.)

My life and career have been dedicated to helping others overcome adversity, to helping them resurrect their inner strength and confidence at crucial, life-defining moments. I train individuals and teams in resilience strategies, focusing on building the characteristics necessary to manage any crisis or adversity. I have worked with, and advocated for, victims of violence for nearly two decades. I have trained thousands of leaders through difficult times. Yet for years I struggled to find the words: the calming, wise, perfect message someone needs in their darkest moments. I struggled to suggest the one perfect action that would enable them to thrive again.

One day, several years into this work, I spoke with a victim of a debilitating attack. Her struggles were all-too familiar: the self-blame, confusion, anger, and desperate need to feel normal again. She spun through her feelings, asking how she was going to work or get married or have friendships or ever again feel safe going out at night. The spiral of grief and trauma had overwhelmed her, leaving her bedridden most days.

"I can't. I can't eat. I can't sleep. I can't get out of bed. I don't know how to do this," she sobbed.

"Get up," I said. "Nothing more is expected of you. You don't have to have all the answers right now. There is no perfect way to do this. You just have to get up."

My words sunk into me, causing a ripple of surprise and understanding. I smiled to myself: *the voice of resilience had finally merged with my own.*

I had learned that when life brings us to our knees, each moment defines itself. Resilience isn't forged through a single perfect message or action. It is beautiful and messy and chaotic and painful. We aren't meant to know the path forward; it is a test of whether we have enough strength and confidence to simply get up. To do the next right thing. To have the courage to hope. To have the tenacity to take that first step, and each step after.

Resilience is built one purposeful step at a time. We get up. Then we walk. Then we run. And then, when we least expect it, we fly.

Julie Lawson is the CEO of Reins Institute, a leadership development and coaching firm dedicated to building resilient, effective leaders. She is the #1 International Bestselling author of *Warrior Principles: Harnessing the Power of Resilience*. Julie has more than twenty-five years' experience as a nonprofit executive and civic leader and recently founded the National Alliance for Victims.

Lisa Nichols

Faith, Not Sight

"Life is difficult" is the famous opening line of M. Scott Peck's book *The Road Less Traveled*. If you have lived for any length of time, you know this truth all too well. While everyone's story is different, we have all faced difficulties in life, and we will continue to do so this side of Heaven.

While never pleasant at the time, without adversity, trials, and pain, it is difficult for us to grow as individuals. Just as a muscle gets stronger through resistance, we can grow our resiliency muscle through life's challenges. With the permission of our middle daughter, Paige, I share a recent time of adversity and challenge, filled with frequent feelings of hopelessness.

Three years ago, Paige began experiencing numbness, excruciating burning, and stabbing feelings in her hands, legs, feet, and spine. She had difficulty walking unassisted and quickly became wheelchair bound when not lying in bed. The prospect of her never being able to walk again frightened us all. She was only twenty-six and should have been in the prime of her life. She was working hard to finish her nursing degree and, of course, this health setback completely threw her off schedule.

For several months, we spent a night a week in the emergency room (ER) when her pain was unbearable. One night we called 911 because we were afraid that she was having a stroke, the pain was so agonizing. We spent endless hours with doctors, who ordered various tests trying to find the root cause for her condition.

After several unsuccessful attempts, God sent an angel to us in the form of Basima Williams, DO. Basima took the time to dig in and walk with us on this journey. She became the quarterback of our team. She referred us to Ramis Gheith, MD, MS, founder and medical director for the Interventional Pain Institute. Dr. Gheith examined Paige and reviewed all the previous tests. Finally, we got our answer: Paige was diagnosed with small fiber neuropathy.

Now we had an idea of what we were dealing with and could focus on a possible treatment plan. Paige was put on a few different medications in addition to a plethora of supplements. Every Sunday night, I would put her week's worth of pills together (ten to twelve a day) into a pill box for the upcoming week.

After discussing as a family and considering our care team's input, we decided to take Paige to the Mayo Clinic in Rochester, Minnesota, just to make sure that there was nothing else going on that we might have missed. It is difficult to get into Mayo, and we were put on a waiting list. This was another time when we had to be resilient and not give up. Finally, after months of waiting, Paige was approved.

Mayo is one of the most impressive operations we have ever witnessed. They are so organized and efficient. For a week, we had an extensive schedule of tests every day, in different buildings. Paige was still in a wheelchair, but fortunately we stayed in a hotel that is connected by a system of tunnels to the various buildings at the Mayo Clinic. On our second visit to Mayo, they conducted a sural nerve biopsy, which indicated that Paige not only had small fiber neuropathy but large fiber neuropathy as well.

For both small and large fiber neuropathy, John Hopkins had some success with an infusion protocol called Intravenous Immune globulin, or IVIg. The challenge with IVIg is that it is very difficult to get approved as it is expensive and in short supply. Once again, Basima came to the rescue by getting us in to see a nationally known neurologist, Sita Kedia, MD. Dr. Kedia was able to get the treatment approved for Paige. IVIg infusions continued for about eighteen months, and eventually Paige began walking with a walker and then a cane. We were extremely grateful for her progress.

All the while, we continued to read and research what other protocols could potentially help Paige. One day, I was waiting at my daughter Ally's ballroom dance lesson and flipping through a flyer on the counter with an ad that read: "Are you suffering from neuropathy? Do you have burning, tingling, or numbness in your hands, arms, legs, or feet? We might be able to help. Call this number today for your free consultation." I couldn't believe it. I never read those flyers, and most of the time if I am not watching or filming Ally, I am focused on my laptop, catching up with work. But not that day. I could barely contain my excitement and knew that God had orchestrated my whole encounter with that ad.

The next day, I called and scheduled the consultation. They described how they had great success with their treatment plan, that it was FDA approved, nonsurgical, and, best of all, drug free. We decided to try it. Two to three times a week, we took Paige in for treatment for close to six months. Within a few months, Paige began to get some feeling back in her feet, which allowed her more mobility.

At this time, Paige was no longer driving and had not driven since she became sick in July of 2019. In addition, she is the single mother of our grandson, Sawyer. The multiple treatments and doctors' appointments and crazy work schedules made getting everyone where they needed to be challenging, but again we had the fortitude and resilience to make it work. It was worth continuing to push for better outcomes for our precious daughter.

For Christmas in 2021, we took a much-needed family vacation in Naples, Florida. Paige said her number one goal while there was to practice walking without the cane. I am teary-eyed as I type this, because while we were in Florida, she threw away her cane. She has been walking unassisted ever since. When we got back to St. Louis, Paige said she wanted to learn to drive again. She began with daily trips to a cute little convenience store five minutes from our home, and gradually expanded her radius. Today, I am thrilled to say she drives wherever and whenever she needs to.

Paige is never free from pain, but she has gained her independence and her mobility, and her hope is restored. She is taking medical coding classes and earning straight A's. She works as a nanny for twenty to thirty hours a week while in school. Although her future looks different than what she dreamed of, she has learned so much from this journey, and so have we. Paige has said she wouldn't change a thing about what has happened. God has deepened our faith and trust in Him, we all have a renewed sense of gratitude, and we are closer than we have ever been as we have tackled this journey head-on together.

A practice we started during this three-year journey is to be intentional about voicing our gratitude. Every night, the entire family forms a gratitude circle, and we all say what we are grateful for. Then we pray as a family. It is a precious time that we all look forward to.

Here are just a few of the resilience lessons I've learned on this journey with Paige:

1. Prayer works! God is faithful to answer us when we call upon Him. Just know that the answer may not always look the way we think it should; but we can trust Him, His purposes, and His ways. (Jeremiah 29:1, James 5:16)

2. God's strength is made perfect in our weakness. If we lean on Him during hard times, not only will we build our resilience muscle, but our faith muscle will grow as well. (2 Corinthians 12:8–10)

3. The resilience muscle can be developed, but it is not easy. Oftentimes, it is in the fire that we grow the most. (James 1:2–4)

4. You cannot go it alone. You need a tribe—people who will cheer you on in tough times when you lose hope. Paige has said many times that if it had not been for the support and the resilience of her family, she would have given up.

5. Never ever give up! Dr. Jason Selk, bestselling author of *Relentless Solution Focus*, talks about problem-centric thinking versus relentless solution thinking. Eighty percent of our thoughts are negative. When those negative doubts and thoughts come, think instead, "What is the *one* thing I can do right now to move in the right direction?" Most people give up before they ever get to the solution, but don't! Keep pushing for answers. We are still pushing for more answers for Paige and will not stop. (1 John 5:4, Philippians 4:13)

James 1:2–4 (NIV) assures us: "Consider it pure joy, my brothers and sisters, whenever you face trials of many kinds, because you know that the testing of your faith produces perseverance. Let perseverance finish its work so that you may be mature and complete, not lacking anything."

Lisa Nichols is the CEO and cofounder of Technology Partners, a Women-Business Enterprise and provider of premier IT staffing, solutions, and IT leadership development. Named among the Most Influential Business Women (by *St. Louis Business Journal*), Lisa's influence has been recognized by her peers and Greater St. Louis.

Lisa and her husband, Greg, founded Technology Partners in 1994, driven by their passion to revolutionize the staffing industry with their transparent business model. Greg and Lisa have made it their priority to create mutual wins for their employees, clients, and community.

Lisa is also the host of the podcast *Something Extra*, which was inspired by her daughter Ally, who has Down syndrome. She scientifically has an extra twenty-first chromosome but has many "something extras." In this leadership podcast, Lisa interviews leaders from all walks of life to learn from them what it takes to be a leader in today's marketplace.

Bianca Strickland

From Teen Mom to the C-Suite

At ten years old, I discovered what I wanted to be when I grew up. It was a normal Sunday afternoon at Grandma's house watching one of her favorite '80s flicks, *Working Girl*, starring Melanie Griffith and Harrison Ford. Melanie played the character of Tess McGill, who was a receptionist at a large corporation in New York City. Tess pitched a great idea to her boss, who then stole it as her own, landing a multimillion-dollar business deal. The story continued with Tess relentlessly proving to these investors that it was her idea, and that she had the skills to be more than a receptionist. That perseverance paid off. The story ends "happily ever after" with Tess promoted to her former boss's position and securing a corner office overlooking NYC.

Most ten-year-old girls would have been unimpressed with the story of Tess, but I was instantly inspired and was certain I was going to be her someday. Fast-forward to sixteen-year-old me enjoying all the things a small Midwest town of twelve hundred people could offer: Friday night football, county fairs, creek slabs, and gravel roads. My social life was my number one priority, and there was no shortage of fun. I was an expert at having it, sometimes a little too much. I was head over heels in love with my boyfriend. I was irresponsible and thought I was invincible most days. I've always been very independent and stubborn. No one could tell me anything, especially my parents, who relentlessly tried to slow me down and keep me on a more responsible track. Unfortunately, being young and dumb went together way too easily, and I wasn't going to slow down or stop what I assumed to be the best years of my life. That is, until life stopped me in my tracks and taught me the living, breathing definition of resilience.

Two weeks before my seventeenth birthday, and after weeks of just knowing in my heart, I finally did it . . . I took the test. Four minutes seemed like an eternity, but eventually the results were in my face. I was pregnant. I had overwhelming emotions: I was scared, sad, embarrassed, but mostly felt discouraged and defeated. At that moment, I thought for sure my life was over. My dream of ditching this small town and being a *Working Girl* in NYC was just that—a dream that would never come true. That was until November 26, 2006, and Miss Tessa Nicole was born. At that very moment, I felt silly. How could I think this beautiful baby was a mistake? I was instantly inspired, and my new dream emerged: simply being a mom. I excitedly traded in my *Working Girl* dreams for a white picket fence with our new family of three in rural America. A year later, life once again challenged my resilience. I realized that at eighteen I was going to become a single mom. I had to dig deep to figure out what my real purpose in life was, because at that moment, both dreams I had been so confident about seemed impossible to achieve.

I spent the next five years pouring my heartbreak, anger, sadness, and fear into working multiple jobs, finishing school, and making every mom mistake you could think of. I had a grudge against every person, place, or thing that stood in the way of the life I wanted to give my daughter, and I was determined to persevere.

I landed my first corporate job at a local natural gas company. This was the first time I felt like we could finally breathe and for once not live financially and emotionally stressed. We moved a few towns away to be closer to this new job, and I enrolled my daughter into first grade at a private school. To some, this may not have seemed like a lot, but for me it was major progress. A few years later, here comes resiliency test number three, when that dream job was in jeopardy. The company launched a new growth strategy, and my position was moved an hour away from home. That meant early mornings and late nights, all while raising a child on my own. As a woman, I was frustrated: "Why do we always have to choose? Why do I have to face this alone?" But I did face things, and I chose time with my daughter and left that secure corporate job with nothing but faith that it would lead to something better.

I felt defeated, and I still had a daughter to provide for, so I pushed forward. An opportunity at a small privately owned utility construction company close to home came my way, and I was hired as an entry-level receptionist. This position came with a pay cut, and I felt like I was starting over. A few months in, I questioned my decision. It was important to me to have time with Tessa at this age, but I feared I sacrificed too much financially. The pay cut hit harder than I initially thought, and I wasn't sure I could afford her private school anymore.

Other than the financial concerns, I was excited about my new job and the organization. The company culture felt like home. It was blue collar with family values and a strong sense of work ethic and goal setting. I could quickly tell I was going to have to make sacrifices if I wanted to grow with the organization and keep up with the company leaders. My personal goals were not to be a receptionist forever, and it would take significant hard work and creativity to make those around me see that too. Like most small construction companies, the culture was male dominated. My boss was the only female leader, but I wasn't intimated by that. If anything, I wanted to be a part of the culture and it motivated me. The Tess McGill, *Working Girl* fire I'd felt at ten years old was ignited once again.

After a couple years of hard work, opportunities began to open, and I was given a manager position. Once I had a seat at the table, I wanted to increase my business knowledge, so I decided to get my master's degree. My coworkers and family thought I was crazy for taking on the challenge, but after three years of sleepless nights I graduated with an MBA.

Fast-forward to 2022 and I'm very proud to be the Chief People Officer of the same organization, which has grown to $500+M and 1,500 employees nationwide. I am extremely grateful and humbled to lead a team of twenty within HR, Recruiting, and Culture. Over the last fifteen years, I went from facing teen pregnancy, being a single mom, getting my MBA, and starting as a receptionist, to climbing the corporate ladder and earning a C-Suite position, all before I was forty years old. Getting here was quite a journey, and I now faced a whole new set of resilience tests within corporate America. Not only was I the only female leader over my 9-year journey, I was also the youngest. As women, it's hard to get past that need to prove yourself at a level that seems excessive. Then, add on the fact that I am half the age of all my peers, and that feeling of constant proposing, proving, and compromising seems even more excessive. I have and will continue to push through those challenges. I am so proud that my own *Working Girl* story became my reality and I, like Tess McGill, didn't give up and did whatever I needed to reach my goals and go from Receptionist to C-Suite Executive. The only small difference: life blessed me with a beautiful daughter to raise along the way.

According to Pediaa.com, the definition of resilience is "one's ability to recover quickly from difficulties." Fifteen years ago, this seemed negative, exhausting, and defeating. At the time, the difficulties seemed to take away the only two dreams I've ever had: (1) having the life of Tess McGill and living my own *Working Girl* story, and (2) building a family of three with a white picket fence. It's funny how life goes full circle. The whole time I thought these difficulties were stealing my dreams, it turns out they were creating them. When I had my daughter, I traded puppy love for true love and grew my career from the bottom up. I even got my white picket fence, and it looks even better than my original dream. None of that would have been possible without resilience.

Difficulties afforded me the opportunity to be a mom, a professional executive, and, overall, the strong, successful woman I am today. I didn't know it then, but through every resilient moment, I gained something even better that ultimately changed my life. Now instead of wishing difficulties away, I embrace them, because I know whatever is on the other side is one step closer to the dream I hold. Face those difficulties, recover quickly, and watch your dreams come true—that's my definition of resilience!

Bianca is Chief People Officer for ADB Companies, LLC.

After joining ADB in 2013, she was quickly promoted and eventually took over the HR, Talent Acquisition, and Culture divisions. With her wide range of experience in HR, Talent Acquisition, Performance Management, Employee Relations, M&A integration, Culture, Strategic Planning, and People Development, she has been instrumental in the organization's rapid growth.

Bianca leads a team of twenty HR and recruiting professionals, serving over fifteen hundred team members nationwide. She has focused her career on providing a work environment that attracts and develops blue-collar workers into future leaders. A forward-thinking leader with an entrepreneurial spirit, Bianca dreams big and is passionate about paving a path for young professionals to grow their careers and make a difference in the construction space.

With more than twelve years of experience in the utility construction and telecommunications industries, Bianca earned her bachelor's in Human Resource Management in 2014, and her MBA in 2018 from Missouri Baptist University.

Renee Moore

Who's to Say?

Have you heard the Taoist tale about the farmer and his horse? A farmer's horse runs away, and his neighbors say, "That's such bad luck." The farmer replies, "Maybe." Then the horse returns, bringing along three wild horses, and the neighbors say, "How wonderful." The farmer replies, "Maybe." When the farmer's son breaks his leg riding one of the wild horses, the neighbors say, "How unfortunate." The farmer replies, "Maybe." The next day all the young men in the village are drafted into the army, but the farmer's son was passed by because of his broken leg. When the neighbors congratulated the farmer on how well things turned out, the farmer replied, "Maybe."

I've seen this story dissected by different business leaders and coaches for its obvious lesson about not falling into the trap of defining situations as lucky or unlucky, good or bad, fortunate or unfortunate. And that's a very valid lesson.

But I've always thought there were more lessons from this farmer tale. Lessons about resilience and not allowing other people to define your situation.

The thing that sticks out for me each time I hear this story is that the farmer continues farming. With or without a horse, he continues farming. With or without an injured son, he continues farming. The farmer is the personification of resilience. The farmer isn't portrayed as a wide-eyed optimist who always looks on the bright side of every situation. And he isn't portrayed as a cynic, defeatist, or pessimist facing disappointment. However, I remember one business coach describing the farmer as apathetic and disengaged with his environment. I openly disagreed with that analysis. Have you ever met a farmer? It's literally their job to connect with their environment. They physically immerse themselves in their environment by working the land, planting, sowing, and growing. The farmer is not apathetic; he's resilient. He continues to farm despite his circumstances. And most importantly, he continues to farm despite comments from his neighbors.

How true to life is it that the neighbors felt compelled to comment on every aspect of this farmer's life? Who are they to say what is good or bad, fortunate or unfortunate? Don't we all have people like this in our lives, who offer opinions we never asked for? The critical lesson of the story is that the farmer didn't let other people define his life. Not only did he not allow them to define his life, but he also refused to engage with them in a conversation about his life. He shut down the sideline conversations with one word: "Maybe." And then he continued farming.

People freely offered opinions about my new magazine when I bought my franchise. Everyone had something to say, and none of it was positive. I clearly recall one business owner saying, "No one is going to read your magazine because people don't read print anymore." I remember thinking, "Amazon started out selling books, so . . ."

When my magazine launched in February 2020, it felt like people couldn't wait to line up along Kirkwood Road to give their unsolicited opinions. "This won't last long." "We already have a local publication." "The people of Kirkwood don't want a lifestyle magazine." "Everyone knows everyone in Kirkwood, so there are no new stories to write about."

"No one will advertise in your magazine because all the businesses have been here forever and don't need to advertise." And my personal favorite is: "You don't live here, so what can you possibly know about our community?" I heard all the people and all their opinions about the hurdles I would have to overcome to make this magazine successful, but I remember thinking, "Who's to say?"

I can't say that I was resilient and snapped back from all their negativity. Honestly, I was too overwhelmed with owning a new business to listen to what people had to say. There was so much to learn that first year in business, and, like the farmer, I had to keep planting seeds to get something to grow.

Someone in the publishing industry told me, "Owning a magazine is the hardest thing you'll ever do." I remember thinking, "Define 'hard.'" I've never farmed, but I've been around enough farmers to know that farming is hard. I once had a hog farmer tell me he could never do anything else because hogs are in his blood. I remember thinking, "Um, gross." Still, I understood what he was saying.

I can't say that owning a magazine is in my blood, but I believe I've started something worth growing. It is hard. But is it the hardest thing? Absolutely not. Are there huge challenges? Every day. And that's not hyperbole. Every day I must face the challenge of partnering with businesses, making connections, getting involved in organizations, working with foundations and nonprofits, adding stories, adding pages, and adding distribution. Those are my challenges, but I knew that when I bought the business. But if I apply the lessons I've learned from the farmer, I know that circumstances can turn from difficult to desirable. And then back to difficult. And then back to desirable. I also know that no one gets the power to define what happens to me except me.

A woman buys a magazine. The community says, "No one will read it." "Who's to say?" says the woman. The magazine launches at the beginning of a pandemic when everyone is sheltered at home. "What a great time to launch a magazine," says the community. "Who's to say?" says the woman. The pandemic shuts down businesses, and the woman loses most of her significant clients. "How unfortunate," says the community. "Who's to say?" says the woman. Businesses come and go, but lasting connections are made, and after a challenging three years, the community says, "What's in the next issue?" "Who's to say?" responds the woman.

Don't let other people define your situation. This is your journey (your farm). How you define your situation is singularly up to you. But really, why waste energy and emotion defining your situation? This is your farm. Dig in. Farming is hard, and you can't predict what will happen. Is it worth it to keep farming? The only person who can say is you.

Renee Moore is the owner and publisher of *Kirkwood Lifestyle Magazine*, a hyperlocal monthly publication that is distributed directly to homes in Kirkwood, Webster Groves, Warson Woods, Glendale, and Des Peres.

Before starting her magazine, Renee applied her business marketing degree to help launch everything from blockbuster pharmaceutical brands to small start-ups. After working with a wide variety of businesses in multiple industries, it became clear that every business has a unique story to tell. *Kirkwood Lifestyle Magazine*'s mission is to connect businesses to their target market by sharing the stories of the people, places, and things that connect our communities.

Kenyatta Holmes

Be Your Own Goals

I grew up in south Saint Louis City and was in the desegregation program. For those not from the area, this is a program where students enter a lottery and, if chosen, are sent to one of the surrounding county's public schools. My brother and I were sent to the Mehlville School District. To be part of this program, we had to get up around five thirty a.m. to begin our journey because it would sometimes take more than an hour to get to our destination. The elementary that I attended was Blades Elementary. This small school was nestled in a quiet neighborhood in a Saint Louis County suburb. This was when I started to build my life in my mind.

During these trips back and forth, I saw many things, but one thing that piqued my interest was the homes being built. I saw one entire subdivision constructed in the six years I traveled back and forth to Blades Elementary. I believe this was when the resilience in me came to life. According to others, I should have failed. Growing up in a home with no financial stability, limited resources, and drugs was a perfect storm. I watched my mother and father in an unhealthy marriage, my mother battled depression, and my father battled drug addiction. We were poor, moved around a lot from eviction, and sometimes there was nothing on in our home but running water. Food was often scarce, but my mother would usually not eat so my siblings and I could eat. As I made my way through school, we had opportunities in junior high to join clubs and stay after school. I signed up for as many as possible to not be home. I realized at a young age that I did not like the toxic situation at my house.

Resilience has been more of a mindset than an action all my life. I had a meager chance of being the person I am today, but God saw fit to hear my prayers and change my mindset. Listening to any motivational speaker, successful professional athlete, or businessperson, they will tell you that their mindset got them further than they would have ever imagined. That right there is resilience! We must change our mindset to be prepared to push through disappointment and adversity. There are things in my life that I could not have gotten through if I didn't have a resilient mindset. Many people see me now and are shocked when I tell them what I have come from and been through. For years, I fell into the status quo of the person I was destined to be by society's standards because I was in a state of depression or, as I call it, a cloud of confusion. But the critical fact is that I did not know I was depressed. That term was not used within my family or home, so all I knew is that I was unhappy with my life. It wasn't until I had my oldest son that a genuine light bulb went off and shaped my future.

I had my oldest son out of wedlock and instantly fell in love when I heard his heartbeat. He was mine, and I was going to protect him at all costs from what I'd experienced in childhood. I would have never imagined that a baby would be the catalyst or a reigniting vision for the rest of my life. When I had him, resilience stepped back in, and my mindset shifted again. I had a hard pregnancy, but I was shown a different light once he was born.

I remember when I took him in for an early visit, and his pediatrician told me that he was depressed. I was so confused—how could a baby be depressed? The doctor grabbed my hand and explained that he was depressed because I was depressed. After watching my mother battle with depression and how it impacted me, I knew I needed to make a change immediately. I didn't know at that time that I also suffered from some of the symptoms. This was a pivotal moment in my life where I would go from victim to victory. I knew the life that I grew up in was not what I wanted for him, but I was unsure how to make it happen. I began by going to a therapist his pediatrician recommended, which was one of the best things I have ever done. She helped me see common trends in my life and family of origin and how to change things for my future family. I also began to journal and set goals, which included molding my career and returning to complete my bachelor's degree. These were instrumental actions that would help me make a different childhood for my son.

My oldest son is now sixteen, and I am passing these lessons on to him. He knows our history and how he saved my life, in a sense. At an early age, I would take him on trips to neighborhoods in Saint Louis County with beautiful homes. I wanted to show him what was possible. We would talk about the houses, what kind of cars were in the driveway, and what we thought it took to get there. I wanted him to know that anything was possible and that his skin color was not the determining factor in his success. But recently, he told me he didn't know how he would pass his government class because he is not a fan of social studies. I told him it was simple: You don't have to like the class to pass it; you have to pass it to get to where you're going. During the conversation, I told him many short stories of things I did not like or care for but had to complete in order to get to where I am today. In his mind, he thought to be successful he was supposed to like every class. This mindset shift needed to happen when it did because that was a recipe for failure. Every time you level up or aspire to level up, I told him, there has to be a mindset shift. You cannot grow in new spaces with the same mindset. The mind is like a muscle: you must strengthen it with the right thoughts, words, and people in your daily life.

For many years, I believed things were happening to me instead of my being in life's driver's seat. I finally got tired of being the victim in my life, and I chose to stop being reactive and instead be more proactive with life. Once I realized this, I moved from survival mode to owning my dreams. By taking charge of my emotions, feelings, and expectations, I changed my course midway and rerouted. I often listen to motivational speaker Eric Thomas, who has a four-minute "Focus" lesson." He says, "To go to the next level in your life, you don't need to do anything, but you do need to do something." Once you get to the point where you are focused and dialed into what you need to do, you will begin to see those changes. This is precisely what I am saying in this chapter.

As I think about myself as a young girl, riding to and from school on the bus, here's what I'd like to tell her: Don't believe what they say; keep dreaming and believing. People would tell me who I was or what I was going to be, and they were wrong. I bet on myself. I would tell her that your dreams will turn into your reality.

I have seen and gone through some tough times, experiences, and emotions during my life, but I never stopped dreaming. I believe that is what gave me hope to keep going. I knew I was born to make an impact, but I never knew what that was until recently when I was asked to write this chapter. I believed and dreamed of the person I am today, who I was going to be, and I was so happy to meet her finally. I am in a steady state of progress, but I am proud of who I am and who I am becoming.

To all of the readers of this book, be everything you feel in your heart you want to be. Do not get discouraged by a closed door; that means that the path changes, not the goal. Do not be discouraged by a "No," for you have lost nothing. Stay on the path. I no longer look to others as "goals" for my life; I have become my own goals, and you can do the same.

Be your own #goals!

Kenyatta Holmes is a natural nurturer, a champion of Black working parents, a savvy business executive, a community advocate, and a Black woman rising. She's motivated by helping others and considers her ability to be benevolent and show up for people in the spirit of humanity a natural gift.

Her story is one that captures not only her ability to be resilient but also explores what life has taught her about shifting her mindset, facing her fears, and realizing her dreams. Professionally, she is a lead product manager at Mastercard.

Kenyatta is married to Anton, and together they are raising two boys—Cameron and Chase. She holds a BA from the University of Missouri–Saint Louis and a double MA from Webster University. In her spare time, she is an active member of Delta Sigma Theta Sorority, Inc–Saint Louis Alumnae Chapter & The National Coalition of 100 Black Women–Metropolitan Saint Louis chapter.

Rose Thompson

Becoming Your Own Hero

"The obstacle is the way." - Ryan Holiday

"Nobody is coming to save us." This was the first significant realization I remember having, at the ripe age of five years old. I recall my mother herding my older sister and me as we tiptoed down the creaky steps of my childhood home in the middle of the night. Earlier that evening, my father had crossed the line one too many times and my mother made the bravest decision of her life—we were leaving. We drove to my grandparents' home to stay the night, and our lives would never be the same.

I felt so much despair and anger, and desperately wished my parents would get back together. At that age, I did not understand adult relationships and marriage, nor did I comprehend my father's struggles with alcohol abuse. It did not take me long to learn that while our new path was daunting, it was better than the prior one.

One of my mother's special gifts is her ability to find joy no matter the circumstances. I'll always remember my mom, sister, and me ordering pizza, watching movies all night atop a pile of blankets and pillows in front of the living room television, or the ever-so-special outings to see movies in the theater with extra buttery popcorn and the bubbliest fountain soda that tickled my nose. It blows my mind now, as an adult, to wrap my head around my mother's resiliency back then.

Imagine going through a four-plus-year divorce process with two daughters living with you full time and attending different schools, battling a combative soon-to-be ex-husband, putting delicious meals on the table, and still giving your daughters opportunities to play sports and participate in Girl Scouts and school clubs. My mother accomplished all of this while working full time, plus two part-time jobs, and attending night school to earn her bachelor's degree. I witnessed her unrelenting work ethic, and how she thrived as a woman and mother against all odds. If my mother was ever afraid, I never saw it. I only saw her bravery.

The first time I felt I had to be brave was when I entered high school. I was a painfully shy child and was terrified on that first day of school. By the third day, I felt myself transforming. I grew more excited with each passing day. Everything started to click; I learned how to manage a modular schedule, I was excelling academically, enjoying every single class, and joining all the clubs and sports I could. I was building my identity as a young woman, and it felt incredible. I was beginning to feel a confidence and independence inside myself that I had never previously felt. I learned that I, too, could be brave, just like my mother.

It wasn't until I tore up my knees from playing sports that I realized bravery is only one piece of the puzzle in life. The first time I tore my ACL, I was devastated. The physician told me that surgery and rehab would probably take four-to-six months. Given that challenge, the real athlete in me awoke that day. I was determined to make it four months or less. I had just learned to be brave at school, and now it was time to learn to be resilient.

I continued pushing myself to the absolute physical limit so much that I tore my knees up even more, which required four more surgeries. After graduate school, I took up running and enjoyed the runner's high, but I didn't realize the additional damage I was doing to my knees.

By the time I was preparing for my fifth knee surgery, I recognized my mother's pattern of resiliency in me. Dealing with my first marriage ending, finding a new place to live, packing up my life, and moving—all with a bum knee—was a never-ending chaos loop. I also threw a career change into the mix. When I was home after surgery, rigged up to a motorized ice cooler packed around my knee, I recall lying there all alone thinking that nobody was coming to save me; nobody was going to show up with a magic wand and make everything better. The only person who was going to get me through all of this was me. There were no shortcuts to any of my challenges. As much as I wanted to keep taking the pain medication and lie on the couch feeling sorry for myself, none of that would get me out of the rut I was in that felt so deep.

I had a long and painful rehab process ahead and did everything I could to streamline it. I was no stranger to hard work. I committed to that more resilient version of myself, the one on the other side of all the turmoil and physical pain. To get past these hurdles, I reminded myself that my challenges were nothing compared to the obstacles my mother overcame.

After a bumpy but successful rehab, I was ready for a new physical challenge. I joined a new gym and started working with a personal trainer. Soon after, the relationship I was in ended abruptly, and I was once again starting a new chapter. As much as it sucked, I had been here before. I knew how to deal with detours, and I honestly knew that this was the best thing that could happen to me. Still, it was painful. I knew pain, and pain knew me, and while we weren't exactly friends, everything on the other side of pain up to that point in my life had led me to great things.

After my breakup, I was an emotional wreck at the next session with my personal trainer. I told him I needed to pour myself into the weight training so I would have something measurable to focus on while I got things sorted out.

I'll never forget what he told me: "You're getting strong with the weight training we're doing. We can accelerate your training and you could be competitive in powerlifting if you ever wanted to try. The gym is hosting a competition this coming weekend. Come check it out."

I had never heard of powerlifting before. It's a sport in which people perform back squats, bench pressing, and deadlifts with barbells. I knew how to do these lifts because my trainer had already been teaching me. But I had never seen anything like that competition—a bunch of people lifting weights and cheering for each other! I went in as a spectator, and I came out ready to sign up for my first meet. That next week, my trainer and I began preparing for my first powerlifting competition coming up just ten weeks away.

I went on to compete in twelve meets over the next six years. I consistently won podium spots, shattered state records, competed and medaled at national events, and earned invitations to some of the most elite, exclusive competitions across the United States. I loved every second of it. My workplace confidence skyrocketed too. The young woman who had struggled to find her voice at board room tables full of men quickly became a confident and even more capable professional. I shook people's hands and proudly told them why mine were so calloused. My growing physical strength allowed me to say goodbye to feeling intimidated by anyone ever again.

I learned so much about life by training and competing in powerlifting. My progress was by no means linear, but neither is life. Powerlifting gave me the ability to embrace the most challenging moments.

Amid all my knee surgeries, my orthopedic surgeon would speak about the trauma my joints and tissues experienced, and then talk about the recovery and rehabilitation process. The conversations revolved around getting back to where I once was physically, to return to pre-injury status. Looking back, I realize that we never spoke about my body becoming stronger and more durable. Powerlifting taught me that resilience is a muscle that needs to be worked. With each repetition, I built my capacity to bear more weight in all areas of my life.

We have all had our life's journey take a turn we didn't expect. Some of these turns are excruciating and heartbreaking. My mother taught me courage and resilience early on, but I spent so much time trying to rush through the most difficult stages of my life without ever fully comprehending that's where the real magic happens. When life gets you down, remember that you, too, are strong, capable, and resilient. Life will prove it to you over and over again. If you really want to know what you're capable of, do not shy away from the adversity that comes your way. Face it straight on and become the hero you're capable of becoming. When you do that, you'll see firsthand that you don't need anyone to save you either, because you are your own hero.

Rose Thompson is the Chief Operating Officer of ButcherJoseph & Co., an investment banking firm headquartered in downtown St. Louis.

Rose holds leadership positions, membership affiliations, and advisory board roles with several industry organizations and nonprofits.

During her twenty-plus-year career, Rose has amassed experience in marketing, branding, sales, and strategic planning for privately held companies, wealth management firms, and nonprofit boards of directors.

She earned both her Master of Arts and Bachelor of Arts degrees in communication from Saint Louis University.

Rose and her husband, Drew, are proud St. Louis City residents near the renowned National Historic Landmark Tower Grove Park. Along with their three dogs Diesel, Atticus, and Loki, Rose and Drew enjoy hiking, traveling, and culinary experiences around the world. Rose and Drew are proud supporters of the Center for Animal Rescue and Enrichment (CARE-STL), R-K Forever, and the Lift for Life Academy's youth Olympic weightlifting team.

Rhonda Gray

Hiding in Plain Sight

I did everything I could to distract myself as the doctor injected the four-inch needle between my eyes. This was the first of many shots of lidocaine to start the numbing process. I still had to get twenty to twenty-five more injections in my head. I couldn't tell if I was trembling because of the pain or because the temperature in the medical exam room felt like sixty degrees. I clutched a pillow close to my chest and gritted my teeth as the dermatologist and nurse tried to comfort me while they finished my treatment. I had no idea I'd be enduring this painful ordeal every month for more than two years.

In October 2019 I was diagnosed with lichen planopilaris (LPP), an autoimmune condition in which the immune system attacks the stem cells that keep the hair follicles alive. Six months before being diagnosed, I noticed what I thought was typical hair thinning. By August the hair loss had accelerated so quickly that I had a bald strip down the center of my scalp. It looked as if I had a reverse mohawk. I tried every over-the-counter hair product I could find to regrow my hair. Nothing worked. My primary care doctor chalked it up to perimenopause and told me it was common for women my age. I felt helpless, scared, and embarrassed.

As a last resort, I researched and found a dermatologist whose website mentioned her extensive experience in dealing with hair loss. I booked an appointment immediately.

Ten minutes seems like ten hours when you're waiting for a medical diagnosis. I'd come in two weeks prior for my first appointment and the doctor suggested she do a biopsy of my scalp and requested lab work. Now I was sitting in a freezing cold exam room looking at brochures about skin and hair disorders I'd never hear of.

The doctor came into the exam room and asked me to take off my baseball cap. I'd started wearing hats every day to cover the progressive hair loss. Even though she'd just taken pictures of my scalp, I was embarrassed to take my cap off again. She rubbed my scalp gently as she explained that I had LPP, and that it was a form of scarring alopecia. I'd heard of alopecia, but this was before Will Smith went viral after slapping Chris Rock at the Oscars for making a joke about his wife, Jada's, bald head. An unexpected consequence of the firestorm of media attention about this incident was an explosion of interest in alopecia.

The doctor continued examining my scalp while explaining the different types of alopecia and that mine was due to an autoimmune condition. "There's no cure," she said, "but we can treat the scarring with steroid shots and start more aggressive treatments to help stimulate healthy hair follicles."

Now I was scared and confused. Steroid shots. Aggressive treatments. Prescriptions for antibiotics and medicine that's used to treat malaria. I was still trying to process everything she was saying as I noticed her instructing the nurse to prep for steroid injections to my scalp. I braced myself while they cleaned my scalp and started giving me multiple shots in my head.

I thought the steroid injections were bad until it was suggested that I start the platelet-rich plasma (PRP) treatments that required them to draw blood and inject my healthy blood cells into my scalp. This was an entirely different level of pain. The injections between my eyes caused two cyst-like bumps that looked like boobs on my forehead. Even with my scalp numb, I can still hear the crunching sound of the needles piercing my skull. After the treatment, I put on a baseball cap to cover my bloody scalp and swollen forehead.

The treatments aren't covered by insurance, so I pay the $800 cost out of pocket each month. But after more than two years of dealing with the high costs of medical care, I realized that this health crisis has cost me much more.

Shortly after starting the treatments, I'd lost so much of my hair that I decided to shave it all off. Because of my shame and embarrassment about my hair loss, I began trying to hide it any way I could. I wore hats, scarves, and even had custom wigs made. It helped that six months after my treatments began, the pandemic hit and we were forced to shelter in place, so I didn't have to leave the house. I wore hats or wigs on every Zoom call, feeling completely self-conscious.

Before the pandemic, I was always stressed about having to cover my head to attend professional or social events. Every decision about where I could go and how I should dress centered around my hair loss. Figuring out how to hide my hair loss had become another full-time job. It sounds shallow and inconsequential when you think about it. But, for me, like for many women, hair is a huge part of your identity. This is especially true for Black women. While natural hair styles have become normalized for Black women, there's still the mainstream images of beauty that make you question if you can be beautiful without shoulder-length, straightened hair.

This was my internal battle. The hair loss started to define who I believed I was, or rather wasn't. I wasn't attractive enough. I wasn't feminine looking. I wasn't good enough. I felt like I just wasn't right.

My attempts to cover up the hair loss only reinforced my beliefs and caused me to retreat further into hiding. Outwardly I was still my typical optimistic, upbeat self. Inwardly, I was an emotional wreck. At the suggestion of my doctor, I did a detox, eliminating gluten, dairy, and sugar from my diet. I was stuck in the house, with Zoom fatigue, and couldn't even drink a glass of wine or eat comfort food! My daily workouts have always been a part of my self-care for my physical and emotional well-being. With all the gyms closed, my regular exercise routine was not an option. To keep me from sinking into a deeper depression, I started running four to five miles outdoors every morning. Between my detox diet and daily running, I lost seventeen pounds. I'm probably one of only a few people who lost weight while sheltering in place.

Once the world started opening back up and we were able to resume some semblance of our normal routines, I was terrified. While everyone was trying to get back to normal, my new normal had become avoiding contact with people. I felt I had to preempt the curious looks people gave me by explaining what was going on. I was thinner with a nearly bald head. I didn't want people to assume I had a terminal disease or make judgements about my appearance, so I passed on invitations to personal and professional activities. Even as I smiled and went through the motions with the people I did see, I felt completely unseen. They were talking to the pre-LPP diagnosis Rhonda, and I was mentally and emotionally in a different space.

My hair loss journey has taught me a lot about myself, and what's most important in my life. My obsession with my physical appearance and thinking I was defined by my hair caused me to become so self-conscious that I lost sight of my commitment to serve others and make a difference. My purpose has always been to affirm the worth and value of others so they feel courageous enough to be the best version of themselves. I've learned you can't be a light to others if you're hiding in the dark. I'm determined to be a light.

Before this experience I wouldn't have described myself as resilient. That's a quality I associate with leaders of the civil rights movement, social justice activists, and mothers who've lost children to senseless violence. Now I see that resilience is not reserved for public figures or celebrities who persist through adversity. It's about ordinary people having the courage to face their biggest challenges in extraordinary ways.

I'm still going through treatments for my hair loss. I still grit my teeth and curse to tolerate the pain. But I'm no longer hiding in shame to avoid being judged. My hair is growing, but more importantly I've learned to love and accept myself even if it doesn't.

Rhonda Gray is Vice President of Strategy & Innovation at Rung for Women.

Prior to her role at Rung, Rhonda worked as a consultant and performance advisor to small and mid-size businesses. She's also served as a nonprofit executive director and educational consultant. Throughout her career in diverse industries, she has excelled at finding ways to simplify complex situations into manageable work that can truly move the needle toward improved individual and organizational effectiveness.

A relentless agent for change, Rhonda is passionate about supporting women in reaching their full potential and achieving the success they deserve. Throughout her career, she has served as a mentor to youth, and volunteers on several nonprofit boards.

A native of St. Louis, Rhonda obtained her bachelor's degrees in English and business from Alabama A&M University. She has a master's degree in counseling from the University of Missouri–St. Louis.

Chris Krenning

After the Fire

"Remind me that the most fertile lands were
built by the fires of volcanoes." -Andrea Gibson

Fire is a vital part of life. It seems counterintuitive, but even our forests need fire. Periodic fires result in a more stable environment, creating forests that are more resilient, sustainable, and healthy.

For the past hundred years or so, most western states have suppressed forest fires. Doing so has made the forests more susceptible to larger blazes that burn out of control. This suppression causes an imbalance in the ecosystem and, in turn, the trees do not strengthen and grow to their potential. Forests that have not suffered fire are dense with biomass, ample brush, and built-up decay and debris on their floors. When a fire starts and cannot be stopped, it uses this brush and buildup as fuel and can create a megafire that can destroy an entire forest and bring risk to people and property.

In the ideal situation, our forests would be subject to periodic, low-intensity fires. This would allow for the natural cycle of nutrients between soil, plants, and animals. Fires are a necessary part of this cycle that strengthens all levels of the forest ecosystem.

These fires on the forest floors would burn grasses, vegetation, and built-up dead organic material. The area would be opened to sunlight when this low-growing underbrush was cleared. Less underbrush would mean less competition for nutrients, allowing more for the trees. In turn, the trees would become more established and grow stronger.

The soil itself would have increased fertility. The plants, animals, and other materials that would burn in the fire would release nutrients back into the soil sooner than if they were to decay over time.

This fire would clear wildlands of heavy brush, leaving room for new grasses, herbs, and regenerated shrubs that would provide food and habitat for many wildlife species.

With the forests less dense, streams would be fuller and would benefit other types of plants and animals. Trees are a critical aspect of the water cycle. In a healthy cycle, the trees and plants would absorb rain and help replenish groundwater and surface water sources.

Some trees are even fire-dependent. Their bark is fire-resistant. Their cones require heat to open and for the seeds to be released. Some require fire for seed germination. Some trees encourage fire by having leaves with flammable resins. Without fire, some trees and plants would eventually die out.

We see the ways the periodic fires help the forest to become healthier, thrive, and stand stronger against the raging forest megafires. And like the forest, we, too, come back stronger when we face the fires that come into our lives. Like the forest, we do not remain the same. But as we face ourselves, we hope to be more prepared to handle the next environmental stress. We hope to be more resilient in our new realities.

I would label myself as an empath of sorts—it's very easy for me to feel the emotions of other people. As far back as I can remember, I've been concerned with the feelings of others. Even when I was young, I had extra concern about others' feelings being hurt. Someone else's mood could easily make me feel uncomfortable. The silent sulker was especially hard for me to be around. Others would say "just ignore it." But this negative energy would vibrate into me. It just wasn't easy to ignore.

If a friend was having a hard time, I wanted to help because I cared about them. But then to separate the other person's emotion from mine was extremely difficult. I absorbed their energy. To try and support someone who was struggling and then return to my life and family was challenging.

Times in large groups were sometimes overwhelming. If a lot was going on, I could find myself in empathetic overload. My nervous system would be wired.

If someone's feelings were so important to me, did that mean their judgments were equally important? Was I fearful to show certain parts of my personality?

Some other difficult parts: allowing someone else's feelings to have so much value over mine, having deep empathy for others and not receiving it back, having compassion and understanding for someone's situation and them not reciprocating this for me, trying to see others' points of view and them not returning this openness. I would sometimes interpret the behaviors of others as rejection.

Through work in therapy, I began to see how I was allowing this empathy to create negative patterns of behavior in my life. I saw times when I rescued others. I saw how I unfairly expected others to treat me how I treated them. I saw how I let someone else's feelings override my needs. The most important part was seeing how I was untrue to myself.

Someone who does not have this overload of empathy has a more natural sense of where to draw the line. Knowing when someone else's feelings are not our feelings is very important.

Seeing where I needed to change was extremely hard. Learning to be different was painful. Giving such passion to the feelings of others felt like the right way to be. I received positive reinforcement for the way I was. Developing a new boundary felt wrong. Pulling back felt like I was being uncaring to those around me.

The changes started in small steps. Insights came in glimpses here and there. They still do.

I have more balance. I'm someone who connects easily with others. I have good intuition. I can now enjoy these gifts and use them to be helpful to others, and I can delineate someone else's feelings from my own. At times, over-empathizing tries to take over. Sometimes it's still very hard. Other times, the boundaries come more easily. I adjust to different situations and different people.

The last few years have been ones of loss. The sorrow I've experienced has been greater than I could have imagined. The loss of friendship, the loss of a loved job, and the loss of precious lives. One life, our first grandchild, a beautiful granddaughter, born too soon, precious Emmylou. The other, our beloved niece, Amber, the first baby my heart ever loved. Amber was the one who made everyone feel like they were the only person in the room. Our family will forever mourn her loss and will also be thankful for our thirty-three years with her.

The loneliness of this time provided space for reflection. I thought about many of the emotional situations I had faced over the years. I want to be someone who's trying to see new parts of myself, to see new ways I can grow. When I'm honest, I admit that I have not always dared to face all of myself. I am a work in progress. The flip side is being able to see the challenges I did confront. When I see the battles with myself I have overcome, I see a growth that is tenfold.

Recognizing that I was feeling unsteady, acknowledging some unflattering behaviors, and being painfully uncomfortable working with change are my periodic fires on the forest floors. Acknowledging my tendency to over-empathize and in turn to take responsibility for my feelings allowed me the freedom to grow.

With the periodic forest fires, there is growth in other areas of the ecosystem. There are benefits to other plants and animals outside the forest. I, too, had growth that I discovered in unexpected places.

For many years I had an inner world narrative that kept me from believing I could accomplish certain things—sort of a limited view of what I could do. And through my work with emotional challenges about myself and other difficult situations, I found myself motivated and confident to do new things.

My husband and I recently invested in a portable storage business. This was more his interest than mine. Then it became a joint venture between the two of us. Now it is a business I am managing day to day. What a delightful surprise! Today I apply my skills in operations, finance, marketing, and customer service.

I thought this business would be transactional. It rarely is! I hear what is going on in people's lives. Being able to empathize with the customer allows me to give assistance as they navigate through their situation. These customers need our storage containers, and sometimes they need information or referrals to other resources. But many of them really need someone to help them sort out the situation, to be kind, and to listen.

I now use skills that were once a burden to me as a strength. The need for a boundary is still there, but it's a little more natural now. Many times it just falls into place.

Today my empathy motivates me to enjoy life more fully. To serve others. To be curious and problem-solve. Today I am proud of my empathy.

"I explain that now, when someone asks me why I cry so often, I say, 'For the same reason I laugh so often—because I'm paying attention.'" - Glennon Doyle Melton

Chris is the cofounder and owner of UNITS® Moving and Portable Storage of St. Louis. She oversees all aspects of the business. Chris enjoys providing guidance and services to those experiencing life's transitions. Chris previously worked in kitchen and bath design. Her BS in Education provides a foundation in training and communication.

Chris has a passion for many charities. A few are the Leukemia Lymphoma Society, the Megan Meier Foundation, Toys for Tots, Finding Grace Ministries, All Nannas Kids Closet, and the Veterans Community Project.

Chris loves spending time with family and friends. Her family includes her husband, Mike; her children, Tom, Joe, Ethan, daughter-in-law Jackie; and her dogs Rufus and Jack. Chris enjoys laughing, gardening, playing cards, walking, and traveling.

Valeda Keys

One Second at a Time

You've heard people say, "Take it one day at a time." Here's my story of how I learned it's all about one second at a time.

It's been a journey, but so worth it and rewarding. Breast cancer did happen *to* me, but it also happened *for* me. In the last twelve years, I've survived breast cancer twice, along with seven surgeries including a lumpectomy, double mastectomy, reconstruction, nipple reconstruction, and preventative surgery (removal of ovaries and cervix due to gene mutation). I also authored the book *My Strength Is Your Strength*, and started a not-for-profit organization, Valeda's Hope. My book is a "Breast Bible" for my family and newly diagnosed women. We carry the gene mutation BRCA2 like Angelina Jolie, which means we have a high probability of developing breast cancer and ovarian cancer in our lifetimes.

I founded Valeda's Hope to give back to the community and raise awareness. One of our main programs for Valeda's Hope is Recliners for Her. We give recliners to women who have been diagnosed with breast cancer and will undergo a double mastectomy or will have preventative surgery. The recliners help with resting and healing. We have delivered more than three hundred recliners, including to the poorest area of Cape Town, South Africa. I slept in a recliner for more than two years due to the surgeries that left me unable to sleep properly in my very own bed.

Valeda's Hope started in 2013, and we've been serving the community since 2010. We work with Siteman Cancer Center/mammography van (Mammograms for Her) for underserved women. The 3D mobile mammograms are held at the local library. A mammogram helped save my life twice before the age of forty. I was diagnosed with breast cancer at the early age of thirty-seven, then diagnosed again a year and five days later while taking the medication Tamoxifen. Tamoxifen is a medication that prevents breast cancer from forming in the opposite breast, but it didn't work for me. I started getting mammograms at the age of twenty-seven. My mammograms were performed every year without fail because of my family history of breast cancer. My mother survived breast cancer twice at the ages of thirty-six and fifty-six and is living her best life in her seventies. I encourage women and men to get genetic testing if breast cancer or prostate cancer runs in their immediate family. To be forewarned is to be forearmed.

With cancer, early detection is the best detection. When a diagnosis is caught early, the prognosis is so much better. There are more treatment options and a better chance of survival. Women whose breast cancer is detected at an early stage have a 93 percent or higher survival rate in the first five years. The most common type of breast cancer is ductal carcinoma in situ (DCIS), indicating the cancer cell growth starts in the milk ducts. This is a good thing! DCIS is Stage 0 breast cancer, which is what I had with both breast cancers. This is a noninvasive cancer, and the atypical cells have not spread outside of the ducts or lobules into the surrounding breast tissue. DCIS is a very early cancer and is highly treatable, but if it's left undetected, it can spread into surrounding breast tissue.

Did you know that Black women with breast cancer are often diagnosed later and have lower survival rates? Black women may start breast cancer treatment later, and breast cancer is more likely to kill Black women than any other racial or ethnic background. African American women have a 31 percent breast cancer mortality rate—the highest of any United States racial or ethnic group. Once cancer is detected, Black women are more likely to have an aggressive form of breast cancer called triple-negative breast cancer, which has a poorer prognosis. If you're a woman forty years old or over, you're due for a mammogram. Make your appointment and keep your appointment. To learn more about Valeda's Hope, please visit our website, www.valedashope.org. Valeda's Hope will continue to win lives where we can.

My energy is never far away from the mission of Valeda's Hope, as I enjoy making lip gloss and speaking to girls about breast health in my spare time. The lip gloss is a unique, winning way to bring breast cancer awareness to young women, and to help women undergoing treatment feel pampered. The lip gloss is vegan and gluten- and cruelty-free.

When I think of "resiliency," a few words come to mind: hard, unfair, pain, tears, lonely. I felt all of this during my journey with breast cancer. Telling my story, assisting other women with the diagnosis of breast cancer, and taking one second at a time gave me *hope*. Taking one second at a time simply means not taking "one day at a time" anymore. One phone call can simply turn your day into seconds, especially if you weren't expecting the call. With twenty-four hours in a day, sixty minute per hour, and sixty seconds per minute, there are 86,400 seconds in a day. I don't take one day at a time anymore because life can change in a matter of seconds.

Sleeping in a recliner for two years because of the seven surgeries I had due to breast cancer meant taking one second at time. I knew it wouldn't last forever, but that also included changing my mindset. I had to think positive thoughts and take one second at a time. Every day your brain processes about 70,000 thoughts.

Through it all, I have learned we must put ourselves first. Genetic testing is also part of taking one second at a time. I knew I needed to take those steps for my future and my family's future. Two important questions come with genetic testing: "Do you have any children, and do you plan to have any more?" This is because you may want to have children and want a prophylactic double mastectomy due to a positive gene mutation. One second at a time. This can be very hard because this may come with frustration and anger. "Why me? How did this happen? What's next?" About one in every five hundred women in the United States has a mutation in either her BRCA1 or BRCA2 gene. A BRCA mutation occurs when the DNA that makes up the gene becomes damaged in some way. Your parents, siblings, and children are the family members who are most likely to have the same BRCA1 or BRCA2 mutation that you do. A genetic counselor will discuss any conditions for which you are at an increased risk based on the information you provide about your personal and family history. Also, as a human being we must know our blood type; this is vital to our well-being. Do you know your blood type?

Finally, being resilient means keeping and making your checkup appointments and screenings even if you are afraid. Being resilient means checking and knowing your body and breasts. Being resilient means not ignoring anything that feels abnormal. Being resilient and practicing self-care is being aware. Being resilient is listening to your body and your physicians. And, of course, if you're not comfortable with your physician, seek a new one. We must be comfortable in every area of our lives. Take one second at a time. This is resilience.

Valeda Keys is a philanthropist who dedicates and volunteers her time to help create a better world. Founder of Valeda's Hope, she is a wife, a best friend to those with breast cancer, a daughter, an identical twin, a grandmother to three lovely ones, and a mother to two handsome sons. Valeda has been a Licensed Practical Nurse for more than twenty-five years with a breast health certification with breast clinical emphasis. Valeda has traveled to Cape Town, South Africa, and Durban, South Africa to deliver recliners to underserved women recovering from breast surgery. Valeda has received prestigious awards in St. Louis, Missouri, including Women of Achievement, Remarkable Woman /Fox2Now, and the Frankie Fuse Freeman Award. St. Louis Mayor Lyda Krewson proclaimed March 27, 2019, Valeda Keys Day in recognition of her work. Valeda is known for her "It's Mammogram Monday" TV reminders. She has been featured in *Redbook* magazine, *Heart & Soul, Breast Cancer Wellness Magazine, Feast Magazine*, and *STLMade*.

Eliza Simington

Getting to Yes!

Resilience is the process and outcome of successfully adapting to difficult or challenging life experiences, especially through mental, emotional, and behavioral flexibility and adjustment to external and internal demands.
(APA Dictionary of Psychology)

Looking back on my experiences as an employee of City Design Group, I know this definition of resilience is true for me. I began in the accounting department and quickly became acquainted with a number of other positions within the company. My interest grew in several areas as I learned more about each opportunity. After stepping away from accounting, I learned that being a jack-of-all-trades is essential for success. I began to master many skills, and my role quickly evolved into being tasked with designing, restructuring, and implementing the plan to enhance capabilities and capital for the company. At the time, being young, it seemed like an easy task to complete. However, it became evident that the task was harder work than first perceived and would take plenty of dedication to complete a higher level of competency.

As I participated in round-table discussions, coffees, and meetings with heads of the industry, it was evident that the female voice would have to demonstrate high-quality capabilities to receive worthy recognition.

Thus, I took the initiative to create strategies that would be heard and eventually accepted by decision-makers to move our goals forward. I had to insist and persist to receive meetings and follow-up meetings to eventually be included and awarded work on projects. I was met with many noes. When this happened, it was difficult not to shut down, give up hope, and retreat. However, my goals and dreams of achieving success were not far from my vision and pushed me to continue.

Persistence was a must to be acknowledged as a credible face at the table. After many noes, "Yes" finally became the answer, and I got into places that elevated our work goals. Even after getting to yes, the road was still a little bumpy, and sometimes it was difficult to move to the next level.

Being in this position, it would have been easy to just give up, but knowing that I was leading others was one reason I moved forward. The second reason, and far more in-depth, is that this business is a family legacy. City Design Group, Inc., was founded in 1994 by my father, Bernard Simington. He is an industrial engineer who worked in the general contracting field. He saw an opportunity to provide a service that was not provided in the St. Louis construction market, especially with an African American owner. He made the big leap and ventured into entrepreneurship. He chose to start his business in construction services thinking that this would be a unique niche in the city of St. Louis. At that time, he became the first African American to start a business in this field.

Our firm started in a house on Chambers Road in St. Louis County, Missouri. The company later expanded into the Kansas City market for more than five years. Within that time, Bernard saw the need to expand the services offered to our clients. We are now a multi-disciplined engineering consulting firm that specializes in environmental, geotechnical and construction services. It is my desire, as the holder of his legacy, to not drop the ball and to build upon this foundation and take it to greater heights through hard work and true grit.

Just as we were getting positive responses and moving toward our goal, we were met with the recession. Like the pandemic, I didn't believe it would last more than a few months or affect the master plan that had been implemented. We pushed through the hurdles of the next several years, and to our surprise we earned higher-than-expected revenue.

With such extreme changes over a short period of time, I was forced to grow and expand personally. The conversations became more intense; managing talent and client performance stretched me in ways I didn't know were possible. The extreme highs and lows I experienced on almost a daily basis had to be met head-on to accomplish them. So much goes on simultaneously: managing operations, finances, cash flow, hiring and managing employees, client relationships, and changing industry standards. As I meet these challenges, I must maintain a calm disposition, exhibit positive attitude and actions, support everyone, and solve the issues at hand with the expectation of not dropping anything.

These challenges are in no way special to me. Most people in the business industry and in life have similar occurrences. My skills and muscles have been worked out and enhanced with each decision we have made, responding to the outcomes of those decisions.

One of our current biggest challenges is the new tone in America of potential employees seeking nontraditional methods of income. This makes it difficult to find skilled employees for our business. Since we are a construction services–based business where physical labor is required— getting dirty and working hard—many of the potential employees look for nontraditional methods of employment first before signing up for labor-intensive work. Though we are creating ways to reach new employees who are interested in development and growth, progress is slow. My current and future efforts will be to find those who will be an asset to the company. This is proving to be a monumental task, but I intend to stick with it until we succeed.

In my personal life I have faced difficult situations too. I've created my goals and objectives only to be set back by those who meant to derail plans. It is the same in business: plans, goals, and projections can be set, but competitors, weather, and resources create roadblocks. These setbacks or barricades stop us from reaching our goals.

Looking back at the last few years, I see that all the obstacles I've overcome are truly examples of growth and resilience. This growth and resilience could not happen without those who have supported me. I am thankful for friends and family who are there encouraging me to continue toward my goals. Their support builds my confidence to keep going through the stress and challenges.

In the business world, I am fortunate to have those same family and friends, as well as business associates, mentors, partners, and senior business leaders who encourage me to not be discouraged, and who assure me that I will succeed. They remind me that I have what is needed to succeed, and that I must continue to reach my goals. Knowing that I am the vessel to carry on a family legacy gives me the boost I need to pick myself up by my bootstraps to stay in the game and succeed.

As I continue to move through my journey in this leadership role, there is one scripture I remember daily: "I can do all things through Christ who strengthens me." –Philippians 4:13

These quotes inspire me to be resilient. I hope they inspire you too:

"I'm not sure if resilience is ever achieved alone. Experience allows us to learn from example. But if we have someone who loves us—I don't mean who indulges us, but who loves us enough to be on our side—then it's easier to grow resilience, to grow belief in self, to grow

self-esteem. And it's self-esteem that allows a person to stand up."
–Maya Angelou

"Life's reality is that we cannot bounce back. We cannot bounce back because we cannot go back in time to the people we used to be. The parent who loses a child never bounces back. The nineteen-year-old marine who sails for war is gone forever, even if he returns. You know that there is no bouncing back. There is only moving through. What happens to us becomes part of us. Resilient people do not bounce back from hard experiences; they find healthy ways to integrate them into their lives. In time, people find that great calamity met with great spirit can create great strength."
-Eric Greitens

"You all know that I have been sustained throughout my life by three saving graces—my family, my friends, and a faith in the power of resilience and hope. These graces have carried me through difficult times and they have brought more joy to the good times than I ever could have imagined."
-Elizabeth Edwards

Eliza Simington is the Chief Operating Officer of City Design Group, Incorporated (CDG), a construction, geotechnical and environmental services firm. Eliza's key focus is to guide the strategic direction of the organization while maintaining and enhancing the family legacy of a second-generation firm, ensuring that CDG continues to excel in quality services. In this position, daily work focuses on developing partnerships with key players in the architectural engineering and construction industry. Prior to her tenure with City Design Group, Inc., Eliza worked as a Realtor with Coldwell Banker Gundaker. Community service engagement included being an active member of Delta Sigma Theta, Incorporated, an active committee member of Urban Land Institute (ULI), a charter member of the Missouri Women's Affordable Housing Network (WAHN), and a graduate of Leadership St. Louis. Eliza gains and shares knowledge of the plans to develop the economic footprint. She enjoys spending time with her family and friends, vacationing, and decorating cakes.

Cortney Dueming

Never Stuck

Resiliency, for me, is about not letting myself stay stuck: in trauma, experiences that are hurting me, places I don't really want to be, prescribed social or religious expectations, painful relationships, jobs, financial woes, loss, or failure. Resilience is always about making my way forward and recreating my true identity as many times as it takes, from whatever in life created the erosion of who I really am and what I really want.

Life is so short, and I want one full of love, happiness, whimsy, and adventure, so I've learned not to settle or stay stuck. To this end, I'll briefly share six takeaways of how I have "unstuck" myself from situations and been resilient in my path forward:

1) It is always OK to change my mind.

I have been expected and pressured to make promises and commitments to many things, by the church, schools, jobs, social obligations, family expectations, romantic partners, and even a promise so significant as my own life—to death do I part—to a man. I do my best to make good decisions, I learn if I am happy or if I am sad with my choices by experiencing the outcomes of my decisions, as time passes.

I have been stuck and trapped by my decisions and the judgment of others many times in my life, but now I allow myself to change my mind. In essence, I'm not really trapped if I let myself out. I honor and give grace to myself that I don't have a crystal ball to see the future and that when I gain more insight and knowledge of a situation, I'm always allowed to change my mind.

2) It is OK to dump the expectations.

I've been shaped by the American Dream culture, rules of organized religion, judgments of others, and, mostly, I've been driven by the harsh expectations of myself. In one particularly painful example, I crawled out of these limits after a very discouraging marriage and traumatic divorce.

There were many disappointing aspects and neglect I experienced partnering with this person who hurt me during our ten-year marriage, but the worst was when I learned that my husband was having an inappropriate relationship. It wrecked me. When what he was doing came out, he claimed he would bury anybody who got in his way. He nearly did bury me. And yet I still had the church reminding me that I promised never to divorce him and that they expected us to reconcile.

That's a high cost from people who did not have to live my life. I was lucky that he immediately wanted a divorce. With the opposing voices of others trying to keep me trapped, I took an insightful look at the expectations around me that ruled my everyday life: All the said and unsaid obligations to my culture, community, church, family, friends, job, and marriage. I started dumping all the expectations that were hurting me.

3) It's OK to accept help and just survive for a little while.

I'm grateful for the love and support of my family and friends who stuck by me. I had quite a bit of fear of my husband and did not feel the restraining order was enough. I functioned at work and was able to take care of all legal matters, but inside myself I was drowning in deep grief. I would remind myself that it's OK to just survive and that doing anything is good enough. I had a low appetite and struggled to see the future; the loss and trauma were all I felt, and it was a deep sadness I had never experienced before.

I understand how people get to suicide. When life hurts so bad, not living sounds peaceful. The desire to un-live brings a hope to feel safe, free, and at peace. To not have to deal with the hard in life anymore when it swallows one whole. The only trouble is, I don't really know what will happen after this life. I have beliefs, but maybe it's not so peaceful after all? That's a choice I can't unstuck myself from. My mind went there, and I'm glad I stuck around, because I almost didn't make it. I hope those we've lost to suicide have found peace. And for those still here who are thinking about it, I hope you get unstuck. I love my life now, and I'm happy I stuck it out through the grueling hard to get here, and I hope you do too.

4) It's OK to be fearless and bold.

I stayed in survival mode, barely living for quite a while. I read and reread all the scriptures. I learned that a lot of biblical people experienced trauma, betrayal, depression, suicidal ideations, and that we aren't really supposed to be making promises because we can't keep them—yeah, God said that. Which makes sense. If he's all knowing, he can make promises fearlessly; but our meager promises are only based on what we know in that moment. And I need to give myself far more leeway than that.

My surviving evolved into wanting to be bolder and more fearless by putting into action my dumping of expectations. I finally stopped going to the church that shunned me for divorce. I made sure I was eating more, even if I didn't feel like it, and went on long walks with my mom. I bought a little house of my own—all by myself—and didn't tell anyone until I closed on it. After much time and healing, I started working part time for a friend's private counseling practice on the weekends for a couple years.

My spark returned and a decade-long dream emerged. I always wanted my own private practice. I worked for many inpatient and outpatient practices full time over the years. In my new freedom, I had no one holding me back except myself. Most importantly, my mind, body, and soul were healed and whole to help others again.

5) It's OK to take risks.

I remind myself often that I am a good problem-solver and I'll always find my way. Without having all my ducks in a row, I decided to take a risk on my dream! I resigned from my jobs, cashed out my 401(k) to help pay my bills, and devoted all my time to my new future.

Bold and fearless, I worked on opening my private practice. It was magnificent and electrifying that bordered on terrifying! And you know what? Counseling On The Fly LLC has been successful every year since its inception in 2019!

6) It's OK to be resilient.

Some of my dreams have come true. Some of my dreams have died. I still have more dreams that I'm manifesting for my future. I created boundaries because I found that some people wanted me stuck. Some people didn't want me to heal. Some people wanted me to fail. I decided to let go of those people and places in favor of those who were my allies in my healing process to resilience.

I learned that though exiting this world may sound freeing when the pain is so deep, if I keep surviving, healing, and evolving in my fearless and resilient efforts, I get unstuck, and life eventually gets better! It helped me not to worry about failure and to just give my dreams a try. I've taught myself to be true to myself and not the expectations or fears of others. Never stuck, I'm free, I'm thriving, and life really is more magical, loving, and happy!

Cortney Dueming MA, LPC, NCC is a Licensed Professional Counselor with a master's degree in Counseling and Psychology in Education from the University of South Dakota, and she is Board Certified through the National Board of Certified Counselors. Her professional counseling experience began with a license to practice in South Dakota. She obtained her license to practice in Missouri in 2012. Cortney founded Counseling On The Fly LLC in 2019, specializing in women's counseling and life coaching. In 2022, she obtained her license to practice in Texas, where she currently resides. She offers professional counseling and life coaching services virtually to Missouri and Texas residents, and women's life coaching services to women across the United States. She is passionate and devoted to seeing women overcome obstacles, live authentically, and reach their goals and dreams throughout all life stages.

Katie Adastra

Minute by Minute

Rare and Aggressive: the two words you don't want to hear with a cancer diagnosis. Unfortunately, these two words would define the weeks and months to come as I entered my thirties.

When I was in my late twenties, I thought I had figured this life thing out. I had a husband, two children, and had recently graduated with a PhD in Developmental Biology from Washington University in St. Louis, the "Harvard of the Midwest." Pretty good for the first in her family to attend college. I had broken the mold and had recently started my first big-girl job at a Fortune 500 biotechnology company. And then I got the news—metastatic cervical cancer, rare and aggressive.

I realized in that moment that someone could feel multiple emotions at once: sadness, anger, fear, grief, and even relief. It was complicated and overwhelming. The days that followed included many trips to the hospital, hours on the phone talking to family and friends, and nights lying awake wondering what I had done to deserve this. Surely, this was the world getting its revenge on me for the awful things I had done in my life. But none seemed severe enough to bring this on, the entrance to the only club in the world you do not wish to be a part of.

I had been through hardship before the diagnosis. I lost family members, and friends when we were just children. I endured heartbreak and suffered through terrible anxiety during my college years—the pressure of being a first-generation college student, I guess.

The summer before my freshman year of high school brought one incredibly painful event. I was trying out for the school softball team, and all my life softball had been my everything. All the women in my family played, and my sister coached my softball team. I was a great hitter and a pretty good first baseman. At the time we lived at my grandfather's house, and I could walk to the field. The tryouts took three days, and the first day was hard. There had never been another time where I wasn't one of the best on the field, so I decided to push myself the next two days.

At the beginning of the second day, we were hitting in the batting cages. I misjudged my stance, and the ball came flying at me and hit me right on the knuckle. I shook it off and tried to keep going, but the pain was excruciating. I limped through the rest of tryouts wincing anytime I had to catch the ball. Why I never told the coaches of the injury is beyond me. At the end of the last day, the coaches posted a list of who made the cuts. My name wasn't on it. I quickly gathered my stuff and rushed home; except I didn't make it. I broke down on the side of the street and sat in a puddle on the sidewalk and cried. I cried and I cried and I cried. How would I face my family? How would I go to school? What would my teammates think? That defeat still hurts. That was my most painful moment, until it wasn't.

The cancer diagnosis was a moment unlike I have ever felt before. In that moment, I both didn't know what to feel and felt everything all at once. I felt sad that my kids might have to grow up without a mom. I remember reading that children start forming permanent memories at the age of four. "Great, mine are one and two years old," I thought; there was no chance of them remembering me. People would try and say encouraging things like "You will fight this" and "Cancer messed with the wrong b*tch." But I had no idea what the outcome would be, so I tried to control what I could control.

During my treatment, I was given a calendar: chemotherapy on Mondays, external radiation Monday through Thursday, and internal radiation on Fridays. OK, I had a plan; I could work with this. But what they don't tell you about cancer treatment is that you can *always* expect it to change. I was in the hospital six out of the seven days of the week. On the weekends, I made frequent trips to the twenty-four-hour cancer care center because my intravenous catheter was blocked, or because I wasn't feeling well. I had bottles and bottles of pills for nausea, constipation, diarrhea, pain … you name it, I had a pill for it. I carried them everywhere, which wasn't many places. The radiation had made me so tired that I was too exhausted to go more than one place a day. The enormity of the situation hit me hard.

I had taken time off work, which was hard. I got a lot of my self-confidence from work. So all I had all day long was treatment, napping, and thinking. On the days that I couldn't get out of bed because the shots they gave me to counteract the effects of chemotherapy caused horrible bone pain or nausea that hit me if I moved too much too quickly, or the days I couldn't interact with my kids because they had the sniffles or because I was just too damn tired, those were the really hard days. Those days are when I learned what it is to be resilient.

At the time I didn't really think of it as resilience. I thought of it as getting through the moments. It was what I had to do. I wasn't any tougher than anyone else, and I certainly didn't feel tough in those moments. I felt weak, fragile, like I was waiting for the next shoe to drop. Cancer involves a lot of waiting. Waiting at hospital, waiting for results, waiting for the treatment to work. It was daunting. But that is when I found out how to cope, how to be resilient. And it wasn't by being super strong in the moment, or about mental toughness; it was about breaking it down to manageable moments.

When I was overwhelmed with whatever the day had thrown me, I stopped trying to just get through the day or even the hour. I began to take life in minutes. These minutes were manageable. I could think positively for a minute. I could breathe through pain for a minute. I could play with my kids for a minute, even though I was exhausted. After a while these minutes added up. I started getting through hour by hour. It didn't matter if I got knocked down again, I would just break it down to the manageable moments, minute by minute.

There are many definitions of resilience, but the one I am drawn to is the "capacity to recover quickly from difficulties." This definition resonates with me because I know I can take that recovery in measurable moments, one minute at a time.

The experience of cancer is not something I wish on anyone. But now that I am ten years out from my diagnosis, I see the gifts that the experience gave me. It allowed me to really treasure the minutes of my life. It made me brave. Nothing was as scary or as unknown as cancer. This has helped me in my professional and personal life to be resilient, to recover quickly.

This has made me a better sales professional. I don't think there is another profession where you are told "no" or rejected more often than sales. My experience with cancer allows me to take a minute, recover, and then move on.

I am a better mother. OK, maybe being a mom has more moments of "no" and a lot more moments of self-doubt and perceived failure. But I cherish my children, one moment at a time. Like recently when I peeked in on my daughter in the living room, in front of the TV, singing along to a movie. Or when I sneak into to kiss my son on the head while he is asleep in his room at night. I can also help them take one minute at a time to improve their own resilience. Like when my son gets sidelined during his football game and the coaches don't put him back in for the rest of the game. Or when my daughter must slow down to walk during her cross-country race. In these moments, they don't feel strong, they don't think they can go on. But that is when we can break it down to manageable moments. That is when you can walk for a minute to catch your breath, then start running again.

Throughout my life, during the times I have really felt defeated and unable to go on—losing a relative or a friend, not making the team, being passed up for a promotion or role I really wanted—that is when I find strength in the minutes. That is when I break down life to manageable moments, and then … I move on.

Katie Adastra is a Business Development Executive and Senior Client Partner at Centric Consulting, a business and technology consulting firm. Early in her career, Dr. Adastra took her love for translating complex ideas into simple solutions into the realm of Information Technology, and since then has partnered on numerous digital transformation projects with Fortune 500 companies.

Katie is a board member and past Chair of the Siteman Patient and Family Advisory Council, as well as a member of the Barnes Jewish Hospital Ethics Committee and a board member emeritus of 3 Little Bird 4 Life, a cancer support organization. She volunteers through the National Charity League, a mother-daughter philanthropic organization.

Katie is often in the kitchen trying out recipes or cooking (and sampling) delicious meals for her husband and two children. A lifelong resident of St. Louis, her family is renovating a historic home in the city near Forest Park.

Jacqui Ortmann

One Hell of a Brick

Resilience. I used to think this word meant to push ahead, move forward, tackle **all** obstacles, accept **all** challenges, and **go for everything**! And then, August 28, 2021, my world went into a tailspin—**literally**! We had one of our normal, crazy Saturdays: move oldest into her first apartment, attend another's cross country meet, dinner, meet up with friends, etc. (Insert deep breath here!) We were finally on our way home with three of our six children, all of us singing at the top of our lungs to the radio, smiling and laughing. Suddenly, my head started spinning and all I could see were a million taillights swirling around. I couldn't tell what was up or down, left or right. I'm not sure how I got the words out to my husband, "Take me to the hospital now!" It was the longest ten-minute ride of my life. I tried to pray an "Our Father" and a "Hail Mary," but I couldn't. I just kept saying "Jesus, Jesus, Jesus" as I waited for "the lights to go out." I thought, "This is it!"

You know you are in trouble when they don't tell you to take a seat in the ER waiting room. I was in an MRI machine within ten minutes. My blood pressure was 219/108 and they were watching for a stroke. After testing over the next three days, I was told I had the arteries of a sixty-year-old (I was forty-seven). I was prescribed several drugs and assessed for multiple sclerosis. My world had come to a screeching halt!

I have always been independent, self-reliant, and the one who took care of everyone else. Now I was scared, dependent, unsure. I didn't even trust my own head, which was still spinning a bit. I am the one who always took the punches and got right back up. I may throw in a meltdown or two, but I always take pride in succeeding despite any challenge or obstacle. But now I was brought to my knees. Forget confidence. I didn't want to be left alone. My body, my brain, even my soul shut down. Lost doesn't even describe it. Fear was paralyzing me.

In a way, fear was what finally got me to stop. To stop taking on every challenge, to keep moving forward, to go for everything, and to stop abusing *me*! My definition of resilience, at the time, left out the part where you recharge, take a moment to take care of yourself, choose which challenges to push through, and realize when you need to lean on your support system. My definition was deceiving and flawed. My definition nearly **killed me!**

For the next three months I watched my diet, including every calorie and every milligram of salt. I walked and walked. At first, I took twenty-eight laps around my yard, which equaled a mile. I kept close to home in case I'd black out. I started walking ten minutes a day, and by December I was up to two or three miles a day, still within my own yard. I took three-hour naps each day. Three hours! I have never been a nap taker. It took me a month to start driving again, and when I did I always drove on the far right, in case I started spinning, and avoided the interstates. I wore ear plugs (even to church) because any noise made me dizzy and threw off my balance. I was recovering from high blood pressure and vertigo. As much as I hated the experience and would never want to go through that again, it saved my life.

You see, I always pray for bricks, because I usually miss the signs and need a brick to get my attention. Well, this was **one hell of a brick**! Before this happened, I ignored my aches and pains. I didn't have the time to feel bad, so I ignored it and treated it as a challenge and kept pushing ahead.

I am a mother of six—four originals and two bonuses. My husband and I have run our company, Ortmann Concrete, Inc., for nineteen years. I have a strong marriage, beautiful kids, and an amazing (nowhere near perfect—in fact, far from it) life! This is another tool I would use to make excuses: "You have an amazing life! Quit complaining!" "One day you're going to miss this!" Well, I was right; I do have an amazing life, and one day I will miss this, but will it be because the kids are all grown and living their best lives? Or will it be because I'm *dead*?

With this health emergency, I've been given a gift. I was forced to take a pause from life. I scared the hell out of everyone, especially my husband, who is my biggest support and my rock. I scared them so badly, that not only did I have their support but they also went above and beyond to get things done. One common theme was: "What you get done in a day isn't what normal people do. But that's just how you are and have always been, so we went along with it!"

Now, during the last year, I've been finding my norm. My new norm is taking each day at a time, recognizing what I can do, what I do not have control over, and at the end of the day reminding myself that I'm enough. I have always been resilient. My degree is in occupational therapy, and I now run a concrete company. Between those two careers, I had the best job in staying home with my children. I have never measured success in status or money, although they will or can come along. I've tried to follow the "Purpose" I believed God wanted me to fill. I do believe that our Purpose can and will change.

Somewhere along the line, I forgot to fill up, to lean on my support, to be vulnerable. Resilience is *not* pushing through without awareness; it's *not* achieving goals at all costs. Resilience requires awareness. Awareness, first and foremost, of our weaknesses. We need to know when we need help and where to get that help. We need to acknowledge, develop, and be proud of our support system. Our support system is the very foundation of resilience, but only if we use it! I discovered I had built one hell of a support system, I just forgot to ask for **help**! We can be humble but still prideful. Especially if we always try to do everything ourselves.

Resilience requires optimism. We must see the possibilities to set the goals. As we make our lives' plans, we must acknowledge the negatives, the challenges, and anticipate them and create our plan. Plans, rather, as we all know even the best of plans will need to be adjusted. A year ago, I was told I had arteries of a much older person, and that I'd be on several medications for the rest of my life. I took a pause. I took one day at a time. Despite my doubts, I stayed optimistic that I could be better. I didn't accept their prognosis. I am now on only two medications: a baby aspirin and my blood pressure medicine, which has been cut in half. I walk eight to twelve miles a week, I weight train three to four times a week, and I am fifty pounds lighter! I have a monthly therapeutic massage and see a chiropractor every three weeks. I do *not* feel guilty for taking this time for myself, as it helps keep me healthy, both physically and mentally. I pray every day. I have standing appointments with dear friends and protect those appointments like my business ones. I cherish my family days and traditions.

I feel human again. I appreciate my beautiful support system, both personal and business, and I'm proud that they overlap. I use this support system, and I give back to them too. Now I do not accept every challenge; I work on setting boundaries on the challenges that won't improve the quality of my life. I set high goals, because it's better to set a high goal and not achieve it than to set an easy goal and fall short of your best. But I give myself grace if I don't achieve it, and I work at the next plan. Resilience is good. Resilience is necessary, especially for a woman in the construction industry. Especially for a woman who is married. Especially for a woman with a family of six kids. *Especially for a woman.*

Jacqui Ortmann is President and co-owner of Ortmann Concrete, Inc. with her husband, Doug.

Jacqui's business recognitions include SBA St. Louis 2019 Woman Owned Small Business of the Year, Arnold Chamber Businessperson of the Year, ASCC Safety Award, and Angie's List Super Service Award (multiple years). She is a 2016 graduate of SBA Emerging Leaders. Jacqui holds an Associate's Degree in Science and is a Certified Occupational Therapy Assistant.

Jacqui loves her community. She is a Masterpiece Award Recipient for the Fox C-6 District and serves/served on many boards including Arnold Chamber, BNI, Cole's Hope Foundation, C-6 Educational Foundation, former member of Black Dress Circle, and currently a parishioner at St. Joseph Church-Imperial.

Family is Jacqui's top priority, and she spends as much time as possible with them. She encourages her employees to rise to the challenge of work/life harmony and mentors them to reach their personal/professional goals. She also looks for opportunities to empower women and fellow business owners.

Sonya Tandy

Miracles Happen

We sat hand in hand in the patient treatment room waiting for the doctor. Considerable time had passed since the initial diagnosis. It was cancer. Now, having experienced the initial terror that accompanies its announced presence, we came to discuss treatment options and plan our attack. We heard feet shuffle outside the door, then the door handle jiggle, and the doctor entered. We both took a long, deep breath. His face did not project that of a positive discussion. He said he did not have the best news. He told my husband that he had Stage 4 liver cancer. The cancer had metastasized from a prior bout with this disease, and we'd strongly prayed it had been forever banished from his body. The doctor's next words took us further into despair. Instead of words of hope and encouragement we were anxious to hear, it was suggested we get our affairs in order. Similar cases, the doctor said, were usually terminal after about eighteen months. Tears welled up as we looked at each other hand in hand. This was not the news we wanted to hear.

And then it happened. It came as it always had before, from my husband whom I admire so greatly—his resilience. My husband said, "I am sorry, but I do not accept that answer." There was anger in his eyes. He said, "We came here to learn of options for fighting this disease and instead you basically tell us it is over before we have even started the fight.

I'm going to ask you a serious question, doctor, and I want your answer to it." The doctor agreed. My husband continued, "Say you're sitting in my chair right now and just heard this diagnosis. Who would you pursue to help you in this situation?" Surprisingly, he gave the name of a very seasoned, world-renowned surgeon who practiced right in our town. He possessed the skill and expertise to address liver cancer cases like my husband's. "If I were you," said the doctor, "that is where I would go."

We left that office with a mixture of joy and frustration. My husband felt blessed to hear words of encouragement that could lead to favorable treatment options. Words of hope. He knew that no matter what, it wasn't going to be easy, but through prayer and resilience we would triumph.

It took several calls and the help of friends, but we scheduled an appointment to see that physician. In our initial office visit, his nurse/coordinator told us not to get our feelings hurt as he did not have a particularly good bedside manner. We said we didn't care and were happy to be there; we were getting a chance.

Once again, we waited, sitting, holding hands, anticipating the door opening. The office was in an academic medical center, so there were many more people in the room with us—students learning from the master. My husband began with some fishing stories (we had heard the doctor was quite a fisherman) and sharing what our former doctor had said regarding life expectancy of similar patients. This time was different. The doctor was confident and reassuring, even saying we had been given bad input on the prognosis. Instead, he told my husband, "You are a very healthy man, other than this cancerous growth. If you are open to it, I can cut this out of your liver and you will be cancer-free. You will receive chemotherapy as part of the treatment, but after that you'll be good to go." Our relief was beyond joy; it was gratitude mixed with knowing we had been given a miracle, another chance to be together longer. We were excited about the opportunity of working with this talented surgeon.

Finally, the surgery day came. After twelve hours of intense surgery, I took a picture of us in the post-op area. I have an amazing picture of him and I together, all smiles of love and gratitude. A day later he was walking around the hospital floor with the excellent assistance of his caregivers. After seven days he returned home. The amount of resilience and strength that this man called upon to get through his fight with cancer was amazing. As his wife, I had the opportunity to support him through this, which was not always easy. He lost his hair but never his determination and spirit. In the end, he was declared cancer-free. God had answered our prayers.

The bout with his liver wasn't the first fight for him. The first round came unexpectedly as most cancers do. He was traveling for work and noticed a small lump on the side of his neck. He wasn't sure what it was but realized something was wrong. At the time, he was working out of town, overseeing technology for a community hospital. He confided his situation with a nurse working in his department. Her caregiver's background kicked in and she immediately escorted him to the emergency room. The antibiotics they gave him were to rule out tonsillitis. A quick trip to an ear, nose, and throat specialist uncovered the truth. His diagnosis was Stage 3 throat cancer. So this was the start of our first battle with cancer.

He immediately started radiation treatments. If the tumor responded, he'd continue treatment. If not, disfiguring surgery would be in order. After the first two rounds of radiation, the tumor had reduced in size by almost half. The doctors were thrilled with this responsiveness to treatments. My husband looked at this as something to beat. He had determination and resilience, and no matter how sick he got or what he had to go through, he said he was never going to leave me and was going to get healed.

His great attitude and faith were contagious. So many of us prayed for him. It would take several months of treatment. He would fly out on Mondays to do his work and do his treatments. All his treatments were at the facility out of town, where he worked, so I never saw the full impact of the radiation. Then he would travel back home at the end of the week and we would spend three amazing days together. I knew that he was acting, because radiation will burn the flesh and the inner structure of the throat. His doctor said he couldn't believe my husband was able to sustain weekly travel. However, he was forewarned that he would physically "crash" at the end of his course of treatment and that he would need time to recover. He lost about fifty pounds of body weight because it's very difficult to eat when it feels like your flesh is burning in your throat. Absolutely everything tastes terrible. He took the last treatment, flew home, and collapsed on the couch. I couldn't get him to eat. We worked hard to fix a lot of smoothies and protein shakes to get him back to normal weight. In the end he made it through, again through his incredible resilience.

Sometimes it's harder to be the caregiver than it is to be the patient, but in these situations I don't think so. I would never want to put myself into his situation or have to go through what his body went through. He made it seem like nothing. He handled it with an incredible amount of dignity, strength, and courage. I can't even begin to fathom the strength it took for him to get back to health. I will never forget kissing him goodbye the morning he was off to go back to the client and begin working again, cancer-free. We kissed and hugged and off he went.

Resilience can come in many forms and presents itself in many ways—some that you notice, making you stronger, and others by just living it. I am blessed to have my mother, who just celebrated her ninety-first birthday and whom we battled two years of living through the pandemic to keep her and my husband safe. All in all, each day we all live our lives. But I have been blessed to be surrounded by three very special people in my life who know what it is like to face life with a great deal of resilience: my husband, my amazing daughter, and my dearest mother. They continuously show me examples of living with resilience and what it truly means every day. I am blessed to have them in my life, and I try not to take a day for granted. What I do know is that through prayer and faith, miracles happen.

Sonya is a Sustainability Consultant and Regional Account Manager for an organization headquartered in St. Louis, Missouri. In addition to her thirty-five-plus-year career in senior level sales, Sonya enjoys serving her community through board positions she's held for several years for two local nonprofit organizations. She is beyond blessed to be married to her partner, to whom she dedicated her chapter, for more than twenty-six wonderful years. She is inspired daily by her ninety-one-year-old mother's gratitude, love, and support. She feels so blessed to have been given by God her amazing daughter. Her daughter, grandson, and son-in-law are such a joy to be with. Watching her daughter grow into a loving mother, wife, and successful business owner has been a joy. Sonya also loves spending time in Indiana with her extended family and with her loving friends. She loves traveling, reading, and having a great day at the beach!

Cory Elliott

The Pivot Process

The lights are down low and it's so quiet you can hear a pin drop. A woman walks up to the podium and says, "The winner of the company of the year award is …" Of course, this is the day I win! This is my dream. But the reality is this: How much longer can you survive not making the money you know you should be making? How many years are you going to have stolen by stress? Do you know your bank account is negative because the client who was supposed to pay you is now hitting you with a back charge because they must figure out how to make up their losses?

Right now, you're surviving by getting whatever business you can, through whatever channels you can. This is frustrating when you know you should be profitable and competing at a higher level. According to an article written by Janet Attard for businessknowhow.com, only about 9 percent of small businesses have annual sales of over $1 million. The other 91 percent are in danger of going out of business because they are cash strapped. I remember staying up nights thinking, "Why does this have to be so hard? Things would be OK if I could just figure out how to increase my cash flow." Increasing cash flow wasn't the solution. I am part of the 9 percent now, but it didn't start out this way. I failed horribly in certain phases of the business. I failed during growth times in my business because I was so busy chasing the ball that I didn't even realize someone else had taken the ball.

I thought given my previous experience—and if I looked like other construction businesses—that people would support me. We had the website, the logo, the offices, and the polo shirts. I looked like a profitable business owner, but in real life I was struggling to make payroll. Members of my team were stealing from me. My family and friends were secretly doubting me, and I felt like a failure. Then I rose during turmoil. I rose because I didn't have a choice but to move forward. Resilience comes from reevaluating every aspect of your life. There was a shift to determine new strategies to making more profit, attracting choice clients, and lowering my own personal stress levels in the process.

If you're going to make a similar shift, you need to have laser focus. Focus on: Your people, Your processes, and Your philanthropy. First, Your people. You need to get the max out of your team because they want to, not because you pay them. They need to be excited about bringing in business. Second, Your processes. You need a way to guarantee the work is exceptional even if you aren't in the building. A business should run well without you. If you need to crack the whip, then you don't have the right team. Third, Your Philanthropy. Why? You need to be part of a cause bigger than your business because that's your purpose and good comes from giving back.

The people in your way aren't just going to move. Which is why "The Pivot Process" is so important. It allows the use of human nature and habits of other people to accomplish your goals. This is how I became resilient. In the early stages, shifting the focus of the business felt like hard work. There were tough conversations between me and the team. But once the pain passed, there was 100 percent clarity about what was needed for a business to maintain a high level of profitability through efficiency, not your hard work.

In all aspects of my life, I have had to be resilient. I remember my father saying to me, "As a Black woman, you are going to have to work harder, be smarter, and people will always underestimate you." So I did all those things and still failed; nor did I have peace. I had to stop and just breathe.

If you're going to see the peace and prosperity you dream of, it starts in your head. We can't start talking about your people. We need to talk about you and where you want your people to go because you get what you focus on. It's two parts: the vision and the plan. The plan is the step-by-step actions that lead to you achieving your vision. Any action that doesn't put you closer to peace and prosperity should be viewed as a time waster. You and your team should only be doing things that get you the results.

No matter how good your team is, they will only go where you lead them. You don't have time or resources to waste on misunderstandings, so be crystal clear. If you miss your target, it could mean financial ruin for you. Your team will get another job, but what about you? Do you really want to go back into the workforce? I don't know one boss who wants to go back to having a boss, ever. It is critical to get this right. If not for you, for your future generations to effectively compete in the world.

Now, pull out a piece of paper and pen to make a contract with yourself ... (1) "I will make the changes to improve my business and make making money easier." (2) "My new revenue and profit goals are _____." (3) "I am doing this for the benefit of _____." (4) "I will not quit until I reach the goal." This starts with you, but eventually each team member needs to make a similar commitment.

Put down the date you intend to start your work before you start thinking of all the reasons this won't work. If you want to increase your chances of success with your team, plan your work out in phases. I've overseen multimillion-dollar projects for more than twenty years. I find it's much easier to track your progress and stay calm when you roll it out this way. Put the date you expect each phase to be accomplished. Now, put it somewhere you can see it every day. One more thing: set several alerts on your calendar so you are reminded daily what is at stake.

Once your personal contract is done, let's review the vision you're casting. The vision needs to be big enough that it's compelling but at the same time simple. It's an ideal state that is so attractive everybody wants in but is not easily attainable. A quest. A mission. A cause crafted and controlled that leads directly to a profitable bottom line. It needs to be done in steps that keep you and your team motivated.

If you want to make the making of money easier, you must energize, retain, and attract people on your team. In today's world, people don't do it because you're the boss anymore. More than ever before people are doing what's in their own best interest. If this were radio, they would only listen to two stations: WIFM and WIAM. WIFM or What's In It For Me? They are up at night trying to figure out how to make more money for their family. Their life's goal isn't to make you rich. They need to see your vision as the solution to their problem. So the next time they're brainstorming it's about how to better your life and theirs.

The other station they listen to is WIAM or What's Interesting About Me. Your company will take off once you have people working on their skills and bringing ideas to the table. However, that won't happen if they don't think you value them. Nothing's better than a "Hey Ms. Cory, I saw this last night. It sounds like it could make us some money. What do you think?" My response is always, "Do some research, get the details, and

123

let's discuss." You should never be the only one up at night thinking about ways to improve your company.

Every NFL owner plans to win it all every year. It doesn't matter what the roster looks like. The coach believes there's a chance to win the Super Bowl that year. To quote ESPN's Chris Berman: "And that's why they play the games." This describes when a team that's supposed to lose pulls out a big win. I approach business in this same way. Resiliency requires you to play all four quarters of the game. Whether it looks like you are winning or losing, the key is to keep playing the game. This is life. You win, you lose, you stand, you learn, you win, you lose, you stand again. On the hardest days, faith in yourself and your ultimate purpose—yourself—is what makes you resilient in any circumstance.

Cory is the CEO and founder of CMT, LLC, a commercial construction company established in 2012 with offices in St. Louis, Missouri, Champaign, Illinois, and Chicago, Illinois. CMT is a CM, GC and self-performs abatement, interior demolition, roofing, and solar. CMT, LLC is a union contractor.

Prior to starting CMT, LLC, Cory was a senior level executive in healthcare operations and construction. She was known for enhancing operational efficiencies while increasing quality and revenue. In construction, she utilized design elements to enhance the patient's experience while improving satisfaction and clinical outcomes.

Cory is the mother of four wonderful children. Cory is an active member of the community and serves as Treasurer of the Community Children's Resource Board (CCRB) and as Board Member for Casa De Salud and the Construction Forum.

Cory has a bachelor's degree from Saint Louis University and two master's degrees from Washington University in St. Louis.

Arinola Solanke

Resilience from Faith

I remember it like yesterday when we first arrived at St. Louis Lambert International Airport. Holding tightly to my son, Richard (Leke), who was seven at the time, I picked up my bags and the few belongings I could carry with me after living in London for more than two decades. On that cold winter day in November, my husband came up behind me, gave me a big kiss, and wrapped his arms around the both of us as we walked toward the parking lot. That moment was when my American journey began.

God bless the United States of America for being good to me. I have a great family, friends, and community support. In the last several years, Vitendo4Africa, a nonprofit based in St. Louis that provides help to immigrants and their families, has played a phenomenal role in making sure minority immigrant woman entrepreneurs like myself have a seat at the table and are given opportunities to grow.

I was born in Nigeria and spent my formative years in London. London has long been one of the most multicultural cities in the world, and many Londoners, like my late mom, were foreign born. More than 200 languages are spoken throughout its many streets. My blackness back then was just a way I identified myself; it wasn't something I had to explain every time I opened my mouth. That's not to say I didn't experience discrimination and racist statements—oh sure I did, and it was real and painful. Though many decades ago now, I had to overcome discrimination and biases as an immigrant student in high school. I was called all sorts of names. It was hard making friends, or even finding someone to hang with at lunchtime, and my poor mom did not have a clue how to help me. It was hard, but I survived, and today I am thankful that as an immigrant parent I have many places I can go to get the help I need to navigate the challenges that my children may face at school.

My American story has been dotted with experiences that revealed a deeper America to me. Living in St. Louis, Missouri, has both challenged and deepened my understanding of my identity as a black immigrant woman. I was new, and I was excited to find a home here. I wanted so much to assimilate into the American culture, but only to some extent. Given some of my experiences, I worry at times if America will be quite that home for me. Sometimes I feel that each time I try to connect and settle in, there is always a disconnect. For example, many people tell me I have an accent. Often, I will return the compliment and tell them how much I like their accent too, but they look at me almost offended, as if to say "I don't have an accent." Growing up, I was taught every human being has an accent of some sort. So their reaction was new to me. Another new thing I dread is simple questions such as "Where are you from?" and "You are African. Can you braid hair?" I'm sharing all this to help you understand my early experience and how I got here.

The decision to start MyEventsCoordinator–Party Rentals LLC came from my faith and discernment. When I got to St. Louis, I saw many immigrant professionals who were very successful. Their success stories drove me to want to experience the life of entrepreneurship as an immigrant woman, even though I knew there would be both challenges and triumphs. To help me prepare, I worked for almost a decade as an account administrator. During that time, I had my daughter and completed my MBA. In some ways, working for and in a small-business environment gave me the chance to wear many different hats. All these helped me gain exposure to the everyday running of a business and taught me a range of skills that my MBA could not have given me. I was lucky to work closely with the company leaders, who helped me understand how business works.

In the early stage of my entrepreneurial journey, though, I felt I had the mindset, "I'm prepared for this." Yet I felt abandoned, alone, and vulnerable. I didn't always know where to turn for help. I had no mentors, and I knew very little about the power of networking. In addition, minority immigrant and female entrepreneurs have our struggles. Sometimes people don't always understand our accents. It can be difficult to secure funding. Entrepreneurs must fund their dreams themselves, and because my network was not as developed, my credibility was sometimes questioned. Imagine starting a business with all these challenges and difficulties. The truth is, part of the reason I pushed myself and refused to give up was because I had faith and believed in the power of a better tomorrow. My faith has *helped me navigate business decisions in good times and bad times.*

It has been more than ten years since I started My Event Coordinator LLC. Since then, I'm proud to say we've organized events for world leaders, won several awards, and we are a certified Minority Business Enterprise (MBE) and Women Business Enterprise (WBE) company by St. Louis Lambert International Airport. I'm pressing on, not because I have all the answers but because I choose to stand for what I believe. I will continue to work hard and to achieve.

I'm very grateful for my family and organizations like Vinten4Africa, which continues to play a huge role in helping immigrant entrepreneurs like myself move forward. They continue to move the needle toward greater equity and creating opportunities for us to grow. Sometimes entrepreneurs are praised for their boldness and forward thinking, yet they struggle. I struggle sometimes—with keeping the passion afloat, and with feeling respected as a woman *business* owner, and so much more. We all know that minority and female businesses are likely to fail from inadequate funding and the ability to retain customers. *The pandemic was* a very hard time for *my industry, and it hit us hard.* Today, *we* have an incredible story of overcoming and thriving. The pandemic taught me you cannot plan for every single scenario in business, but you can always **be prepared for the unexpected.**

What I do know is that we cannot live in crisis forever. We overcame it and are thriving, and so will you!

Arinola Solanke is the CEO and founder of MyEventsCoordinator–Party Rentals LLC, an events management and party rental company. She is a passionate events and party rental consultant, known for her creative flare and diverse clientele. In 2019, MyEventsCoordinator was certified by the City of St. Louis with the dual local Minority and Women Business Enterprise (MBE/WBE) certifications.

Before founding MyEventsCoordinator, Arinola worked as a financial liaison with the City of Westminster in London, England. She holds an undergraduate degree from London Metropolitan University and earned her Master's in Business Administration from Webster University in St. Louis.

MyEventsCoordinator has sponsored several charitable nonprofit fundraising events including Kookin for Kids by the St. Vincent Home for Children, Youth and Family Center, and Vitendo4Africa, an advocacy organization for St. Louis's African immigrant population.

A member of The Hill community, Arinola enjoys traveling across the United States with her family, and spending time in St. Louis's many beautiful parks.

Karon McCoy

Never Give Up on
Your Dreams and Aspirations

When an educator told my parents that I had a learning disability in math and that they wanted to hold me back a year, I felt defeated and stupid. Yet, despite this disability, I managed to graduate high school with the rest of my class, as scheduled. My experience is one reason why you should never let anyone else's opinion of your capabilities keep you from working toward your goals. Do not allow others' beliefs or negativity to make you feel incapable, or you will never be able to achieve your goals.

Both of my parents only went to school through the eighth grade, but they both had successful careers. Like many other young women, I knew college was not for me; I did not want to face any more humiliation in the classroom. I realized I would never be able to see my dream of becoming an equine veterinarian, due to the science and math involved in attaining that degree. I had no real direction in my life and I was working at a fast food restaurant. This job, I knew, would not be my life's work. At the age of nineteen, I met a young man who was also nineteen years old, and we became engaged. He joined the army and immediately got notice that he would be stationed in Germany. I followed him there, and we married in Denmark. We lived in a third-floor efficiency apartment, which rented for $100.00 per month. I had to carry my bicycle up and down those three floors, just to get to my job on base at a religious bookstore. Talk about character building on so many levels! While in Germany, we visited several other countries and immersed ourselves in their cultures. I gained a real appreciation for this land of "milk and honey" that we call the United States of America. My love for travel and exploration was born from this experience.

Though this marriage did not last seven years, I appreciated my European travel, the people I met, the mental strength I gained, and the job opportunities along the way. From my experience working for the military in Germany, I landed a government job in St. Louis, Missouri. I knew this could be my ticket to a great career, despite the hurdles of my mathematics learning disability. It was about this time that my mother earned her GED and started taking college courses geared toward an associate's degree, all as a divorced, single woman. My mom's accomplishments are another example that no matter how many adversities, challenges, and hurtles life throws your way, you can use them in a positive or negative way. These hurdles will more clearly define your path to reach your goals.

Working for the government without a college degree had its challenges, but it afforded me the ability to move to different government agencies without losing any benefits, and to work my way up the proverbial ladder. I started my government career as a General Services (or GS-3) with the Farmers Home Administration as a file clerk. After two years and little opportunity for a promotion, I accepted a position with the Department of Defense. Being in an agency run by men in those years really had its trials. In several instances, I would have to cover meetings for my male, mostly college educated counterparts. They would come back from lunch inebriated, unable to present their portion of the meetings. Our supervisor would send me in to present instead. Sometimes men would prepare for meetings in the men's restroom, thereby excluding me when I was expected to give a portion of the training. While these male coworkers' antics angered me, I prepared my segment on my own. This kind of adverse work environment gave me the resilience I needed to move forward in my career.

Around this time, my grandmother passed. In her will, she left all her grandchildren $4,000, and I was blessed to be one of ten beneficiaries. In reading my grandmother's final wishes and will, I realized she was a financial wizard: she had invested in the stock market when the time was right, put money in a savings account when it was paying the best interest rates, and purchased bonds when they provided the highest yield. My grandmother was a single mother of three boys, whom she raised on a single salary she earned as a graphic designer for Universal Match Company, despite her limited education. She was a self-made woman and was self-taught in financial strategy! I put this money into a savings account until I could determine how best to honor the woman who gave so graciously.

I had recently remarried a wonderful man who shared my love of travel and had an amazing respect for women. He is a middle child of three sisters, and he and his father were the only males in his household. We talked over this $4,000 gift and what would best honor my grandmother. I had also just changed government agencies to the Social Security Administration because there had been a reduction in force that was threatening my job (no stress there). Besides case technicians, my new agency employed paralegals and attorneys. While working here, I found my calling. I enjoyed the work I was doing, and it was there that the possibility to advance my career appeared. I just happened to see an advertisement from Missouri Baptist University about a condensed paralegal course that was only nine months long, as opposed to the two-year courses offered by other local community colleges. Since it was the length of a pregnancy, surely I could handle that, I reasoned. And did I mention that the tuition for the nine-month certificate was exactly $4,000? Thank you, Grandmother!

This condensed certificate course demanded all my time outside of work. During forty-hours work weeks at Social Security, I would attend college from 4:00–9:00 p.m. four nights a week. I did my homework and studies during my downtime throughout the week and on weekends. Also, a close family member needed my care many days of the week, which took me away from my regular job or my extra study time. It was grueling and daunting, but I knew to succeed I had to persevere and draw on my resilience. After finishing the formal education and the required ninety hours of official non-compensated paralegal work, I received my para-legal certificate. Out of the twenty-five students from orientation, only about fifteen of us managed to graduate.

As you may have heard, the wheels of government turn very slowly, and that was no exception when it came to my career. I applied for many paralegal jobs, in many different cities. Since travel was in our blood, I applied for and was selected for a lateral move across the country with the opportunity to become a paralegal once I proved myself. Sadly, this region felt the need to hire only attorneys to do the paralegal's work of writing disability decisions. After seven years and no promotion, I requested a lateral transfer to another office clear across the country, with the same intent. After a short time, I was offered a computer specialist position on a temporary basis. My expertise is not in computers, but I told the office manager that I would do the job for the benefit of the office.

Through this exhausting temporary assignment of working well past midnight several nights to make sure all the computers and servers would be up and running for the next workday, the Chief Administrative Law Judge noticed my resilience. When I applied for the next paralegal opening offered in that office, my past performance qualified me to be their first choice.

It took ten years, a very supportive husband, a generous grand-mother, a wonderful role model in a mother, and many long days and nights, but I finally achieved my goal. I worked hard to make sure that I wrote enough disability decisions to keep up with my attorney peers, and I often exceeded them!

There will be times when doubts creep in and you feel like you may not succeed, but do not give up. There were times when I questioned my plan, but I am glad that I did not listen to the negative voices from my past. Do not be afraid to step out of your comfort zone to achieve your best. It may not happen when you want it, but if you stick to your plan, and are willing to adjust as needed, you can use your resilience to achieve your higher goals.

In addition to her paralegal certificate, Karon McCoy holds the equivalent to an associate degree. During her thirty-eight-year government employment service, she received many awards, including a Deputy Commissioner's Award for the quality and quantity of the disability decisions she wrote, and she trained new Administrative Law Judges to write disability decisions. She was also awarded one of the highest monetary suggestion awards through the Department of Defense while working for the Army Records Center.

Karon's passion is training dogs, specifically American Staffordshire Terriers. She has placed numerous titles on her dogs, but her favorite has been putting Therapy Dogs certificates on four of her dogs. She adores taking these dogs to nursing homes, hospitals, children's schools, and libraries, bringing smiles to those who are in need. She also relishes breed education. Karon and her husband enjoy rehabbing homes, reviving old vehicles, and traveling.

Helen Jardine

Gifts in Wounds

I remember the blood-stained towels as I stood next my mother's bed. "Women bleed after having a baby," the doctor told her on the phone. "Really nothing to worry about." Then that night, the ambulance came to our home. The female police officer had her gun raised, pointed at my father when he answered the door, knowing only that he had called saying, "Please send help! My wife is bleeding to death!"

I opened my bedroom door. The hall lights were somewhat blinding compared to the darkness of the bedroom. I saw my mom lying on the gurney. As the paramedics were rolling her out, she said, "Everything is going to be OK. Go back to bed." I dutifully closed the door, engulfed in the inky black stillness. I was four and a half years old.

After a hysterectomy and blood transfusions during a week or more stay in the hospital, my mom came home. Our lives were changed forever.

I'm not sure if nature or nurture is more impactful in molding us as we eventually grow into the person we become; however, I do know that as we move through life and its twists and turns, we have choices. I am grateful that events do not need to define us by holding us "known by that experience". In essence, we do not need to be trapped by old beliefs about ourselves based on memories, outdated labels, or projections put on us by others. Rather, what happens to us can help define and shape us into who we choose to become if we allow it and consciously choose to engage in the process of our own evolution as a person.

That initial experience shaped me from an early age to take on a lot of responsibility in our family in the form of caretaking and household duties. There was also living with the uncertainty of my mother's health issues. At a moment's notice, our family might be disrupted and my plans abandoned, as I may have been needed to make dinner, do laundry, or care for my younger brothers or the foster babies we took into our home.

Later in life, I met a woman whose mother had also hemorrhaged after having a child. Our moms would have been about the same age, only our stories had different outcomes. Her mother hemorrhaged during a New York snowstorm, and the ambulance didn't get to her in time.

Each situation can hold its own gifts and wounds to shape us. At some point, we have the choice to become the potter and form the clay of our lives.

Although I did not recognize the gifts as a child and teenager, now having grown into adulthood, through reflection and perspective, I see how this experience helped lay the groundwork for giving me unique gifts—almost like superpowers—that have helped me face adversity with resilience and come out the other side.

From an early age, I learned time management, possibility thinking, foresight, creativity, how to balance multiple priorities, how to look for a silver lining, and I realized that it could be worse; if it doesn't kill you, it makes you stronger. I learned I am stronger than I think and that I am not alone.

These realizations and skills gave me the courage and drive to graduate college in three years and to take my extra year to volunteer in East Los Angeles as a fifth-grade teacher. It also gave me the perseverance and resilience to complete the whole year, when after the first ninety days I found myself questioning my decision and sanity after numerous illnesses, a trip to the LA Free Clinic on Los Angeles public transportation, and a wild attempt to reteach myself every fifth-grade subject. I lesson-planned, checked homework, created tests, and tried to keep the students engaged in learning, while also making sure drug dealers were not approaching them during recess. Then one day I asked a student why he had not completed his homework. "We spent the night on the floor because there were gunshots in our neighborhood," he said. He completed the homework during recess, and I stayed the full year of teaching.

These experiences gave me the confidence to start my own company at the age of twenty-four. With three male business partners, we launched a bilingual video production company after getting downsized by our former employer. Then I switched careers thirteen years later in my late thirties and moved from an industry I knew and had gone to school for into a career in the financial services industry.

As I've surfed the waves of life's ups and downs, I have grown to understand that I do not have to be defined by circumstances or events. I can choose to move through, rise up, and succeed, whether it's overcoming the daily curveballs of life or encountering a more serious life event.

Resilience is drawing upon the internal strength of the human spirit that gives one the ability to get back up when knocked down by life. When we can tune into that true essence of who we are, it shines a light in the darkness like a beacon home, giving us the ability to come back, get up again and again, reinvent, pivot, zigzag, learn, grow, transform, become, evolve, and rise like a phoenix from the ashes. These moments of hardship are then transformed into jewels on a crown of self-empowerment as we discover and own who we are and what we are made of.

These insights have come over time and have helped me to reflect on the events I have experienced. One way to reflect on life's experiences is to

139

journal. Journaling helps me get out of my own head. It's often helpful to "brain dump" feelings and thoughts onto paper just to get them out. Once the experiences are less raw, taking the time to slow down and do reflection journaling can help us gain the gifts from the experiences. Journaling has helped me recognize the many times I've been resilient in life. Maybe you'd like to try?

One way to start journaling is to ask yourself, "What am I really good at?" List all the skills and talents you have. We often think, "If I can do it, everyone must be able to do it." Chances are that your story and experiences have given you unique gifts and talents that only you can bring into the world in your own way.

For example, maybe you popped out of the womb being hilarious (cute baby expressions do bring a smile to people's faces), or maybe you fine-tuned your comedic timing and quick wit by defusing intense family drama with humor?

Finding these treasures is a bit like going on an Indiana Jones adventure. Sometimes the memories are like spears being thrown at you, or waves of emotions can feel like going over a waterfall in a rickety life raft. And then, the glimmers of insights from the aha moments are the beautiful gems of self-discovery.

In addition to freewriting about an experience, and identifying what you're good at, you could list several different life events. Pick one and dive in. How has it shaped you? Explore a series of events: Are you seeing any patterns forming, or multiple strengths being revealed? What can you apply going forward?

Here are some more prompts for journaling:
- What do you want to start doing, keep doing, stop doing? This can help you know when to keep going in a direction and when to pivot to another possible solution.

- Complete the sentence: I am better because of this experience in the following ways ...

- Complete the sentence: I am grateful for this experience because ...

These are just some starter questions as you begin to follow your own path. Taking the time to slow down, journal, meditate, and reflect has helped me get in touch with, appreciate, celebrate, and harness the resiliency of my human spirit. It has also helped me see resilience in others.

My mother passed away in 2017. When she was in the hospital ICU, the doctors discovered that she also had hepatis, likely from the blood transfusions she received all those years ago when she had been hemorrhaging, since they did not test blood as rigorously as they do now. She had been living with it undiagnosed for all those years, although she had been treated for many other health issues that, upon reflection, may have been symptoms of this disease.

What this taught me is that while we can't go back and change the past, we can savor the gifts from our experiences, if we choose. One of my favorite memories is also the picture we used for my mom's celebration of life memorial. In the photo, she's age seventy, with her hands on her hips and a big smile on her face, ready to zipline for the first time. That image, to me, embodies the resiliency of the human spirit.

Helen Jardine, CLU˚, ChFC˚, CFP˚, CASL˚, RICP˚, CLF˚ is the first female District Director with Northwestern Mutual in St. Louis. In addition to helping clients put plans in place to achieve their financial goals and dreams, she has the privilege of selecting and training talented people who are seeking a career with impact and want to make our communities *the* most financially secure in the world. She loves coaching people to help them develop and achieve their potential.

Prior to joining Northwestern Mutual, she was a co-owner of Cor Productions, Inc., a bilingual video production and marketing company located in St. Louis, Missouri. She has also founded and run two women's networking and mastermind groups.

Outside the office, she enjoys spending time with her family and friends. She and her husband, Bill, have been married since 1997. They have two children, Danielle and Tyler. .

Lucinda Perry Jones

On the VERGE of Resilience

On a beautiful fall afternoon, my husband Matt and I embarked on a leisurely hike in the Santa Fe National Forest. As we basked in the tranquility, the trail led us to a rocky incline gnarled with tree roots. My husband quickly scaled it, and I followed his lead. However, a combination of my slippery tennis shoes and clumsiness caused me to tumble mid-stride. I went from a happy hiker to a face-plant in a split second. Because my hands did not break my fall, I fell directly on my chest. I gasped for air but could not draw a breath. My world started to spin. Eventually, oxygen flowed back into my body while Matt quickly surveyed the damage. My right shin was bleeding profusely, thanks to falling on a sharp rock, and I felt incredibly nauseated. Apart from those symptoms and my wounded pride, I was unharmed. After several minutes passed, I was able to stand. Fortunately, the trail's end was near, and I limped back to the car. Lesson learned: never go on hikes without sporting the proper footwear!

I share that story, which I laugh about now, as an example of how change can feel. Whether it is invited or unexpected, change has the power to knock the breath out of us, causing us to lose equilibrium. As we adjust to our new reality, we may also experience heartbreak, disappointment, or anger. How quickly we regain our center of gravity in the wake of change to create a different narrative that aligns with our present circumstances indicates resilience. Essentially, a resilient individual recovers and adapts to his or her current situation with a newfound sense of purpose and perspective.

Given life's rapid cycle of change and unexpected pitfalls, exercising resilience is essential. A body of research shows that resilience can be learned with intentional practice. How we view the world, the quality of our social connections, and coping strategies also support resilience. An analogy I use to describe resilience equates to training for a marathon. Serious marathoners stick to a regimen that combines mindset and supporting behaviors to acquire stamina. These practices often include vigorous workouts, hiring a coach, proper nutrition, support from family and friends, and pure determination to push through fatigue. Likewise, building resilience requires an intentional process. Resilience is only strengthened when we are consistently tested and stretched. As a result, facing adversity and obstacles head-on becomes the workout routine to showcase our toned resilience muscles.

As a transformational change consultant and researcher, I am fascinated by how organizational leaders nurture team resilience. What practices must leaders and teams initiate and adopt to inspire innovation and creativity that often requires change? Amid crisis or failure in the change initiative, how might leaders apply influence effectively so that team members bounce back faster and with increased confidence? In response to these questions, I developed the VERGE model based on research and my professional experience. VERGE stands for **Values, Envision, Reflection, Gratitude,** and **Execution.** When organizations employ the VERGE model, they report increased engagement, deeper connection with teammates, and genuine enthusiasm for reaching the goals they created. These are the same outcomes that help to build resilience.

Values

- Since entering the workforce in the late 1980s, I have never seen so many of my friends and colleagues making such significant career shifts. Nor have I heard so many leave their current positions for organizations that better align with their values.

- Values act as the bridge between the beliefs we hold dear and our behaviors. I define values as our unique internal operating system, helping to organize our inner dialogue as we decide how to think and react. Knowing our values and living authentically reminds us to stay true to ourselves in times of happiness and hardship.

- In an organizational setting, values must be more than aspiring words displayed artistically on conference room walls. Team members become dispirited when they encounter practices, policies, and actions that contradict professed organizational values. However, when values are clearly defined and modeled by everyone, they become touchstones and part of the organizational DNA. To make values come alive with my clients, I implement the following framework:

Carve out the time and space to codesign organizational values with the entire staff. Through facilitated exercises and small groups, I engage the team to share their personal and professional values. Then, we examine where those values converge. For example, if several members cite "curiosity" as a value, that signals a need to dig more deeply into what "being curious" means to the organization.

Assign mindset and behaviors to each value. The group agrees on the top five or six core values to embrace, then they identify the mindset and behaviors that exemplify each value. I also ask them to clarify the behaviors that are out of alignment. The next step is to examine all organizational policies and operations to ensure they support the core values, mindset, and behaviors as they take root and flourish.

Incorporate values into meetings and performance reviews. For values to gain traction, everyone must be accountable for upholding them. When publicly or privately praising staff members, mention the specific behavior and value exhibited. It not only honors the individual but also points out that behavior is desirable to replicate.

Homing in on organizational values is an excellent way to cultivate resilience. When the team has the support and permission to embody organizational values daily, many possibilities emerge, including increased feelings of effectiveness and harmony among leaders, teams, and individuals.

Envision

- When I work with organizations to build strategy, one of the most important and exhilarating activities is discovering the future that wants and needs to emerge. Ideally, every team member participates in envisioning exercises, regardless of their position. Typically, the room buzzes with engagement and connection. Outcomes include increased ownership and accountability for achieving the vision. Since dreaming together produces such stellar results, why wait for a strategic planning process that may only occur every three to five years? I coach leaders to motivate and engage teams and other stakeholders year-round by embedding the following activities:

- **Set aside "sandbox" time for cross-functional department collaboration.** Often, teams are so absorbed in working in their silos that there is little or no interaction with other departments. To foster enhanced cooperation, I suggest regularly convening cross-functional teams and giving them a specific problem to solve. The leader's responsibility is to incorporate the proposed solutions, and to remove barriers that could hamper the desired outcomes suggested by the team. When a crisis hits, the organization will already have a foundation of confidence, creative problem-solving, and the ability to course-correct.

- **Create an Innovation Fund.** Great ideas cannot always wait for the next round of budgets or grant funding. An Innovation Fund is a tangible way for the CEO and leadership team to proactively prevent stagnation. Team members gain experience in presenting a start-up business concept and advocating for their ideas. Of course, not every funded idea will be a home run. However, encouraging team members to experiment with fresh approaches will increase tolerance for failure, allowing the resilience muscle to be flexed.

Reflection and Gratitude

- A top leadership skill that activates mindfulness is the generative cycle of reflection and gratitude. Reflection is a vital grounding tool that moves me from autopilot to a higher level of consciousness. Similarly, my sense of wellbeing is heightened when I take stock of the people and simple pleasures that bring me joy.

- **Take time to reflect.** Individuals, teams, and the organization will benefit when reflection and mindfulness become part of the culture. Reflection might be gained from facilitated discussions, question prompts, writing, or other creative outlets. Most critical to this process is trust-building so that people feel safe to share their concerns and mistakes honestly and openly without fear of retaliation. And don't forget to celebrate the wins too, even the small ones!

- **Appreciate the small stuff.** Dealing with serious life issues can deplete us, making it hard to find a silver lining in the storm clouds. When that is the case, jot down the simple pleasures that came your way. Add sensory words to your list that conjure up the five senses. Or say "thank you" to a stranger or a colleague who did a small favor for you. They will appreciate being seen, and you will activate the cycle of giving and receiving.

Execution

Similar to lifting weights, the VERGE model bears fruit with repetition and refinement. Not only is VERGE effective for organizations and teams, but the framework can be adapted by individuals seeking clarity as they prepare for or recover from change.

Accepting or seeking change inherently carries risks. Chances are we will lose our footing and take an embarrassing plunge at some point, like I did on the hiking trail. To lessen the impact, the VERGE model helps organizations and individuals rise to a stronger state of resilience and transformation.

Contrary to popular myth, Lucinda believes that curious cats live long, interesting lives.

Lucinda Perry Jones, Ed.D. delights in sharing her breadth of experience and collaborating with incurably curious change makers. A versatile and adaptable leader, Lucinda has held positions in the nonprofit, government, and corporate sectors where she specialized in leading program management, policy and advocacy, and philanthropy teams.

As a recognized nonprofit thought leader, Lucinda has been interviewed by KTVI, KMOV, KSDK, KETC, the *St. Louis Post-Dispatch*, *FEAST* Magazine, and *Leading Up for Women*. She has also been a guest speaker on several radio spotlights and podcasts.

Lucinda holds a Doctor of Education in Organizational Leadership from the University of Massachusetts Global. Her research examines how nonprofit CEOs lead as influencers to attain organizational impact. She earned a Master of Public Administration from Saint Louis University and a Bachelor of Arts degree in Theatre Performance from the University of Missouri–Columbia.

Kate Mansker

Long Nights

My mind wandered. What was I doing? Brushing someone's long hair? My hands were swooping in front of me in a repetitive motion, so it was possible. Was I at work? There were several linear flashes of light reflections that resembled conveyor belts, running side to side. Back on planet Earth, neither was correct. I was in an ultramarathon paddling race on the Missouri River. Why was I losing my bearings with the physical world? Answer: sleep deprivation paired with physical exertion over multiple days and nights.

The year was 2008. It was night number two of a nonstop canoe race covering 340 miles. Instead of the latest nail polish color, my hands sported blistered palms that were transitioning to callouses. Earlier that day, I approached a checkpoint boat ramp to resupply after paddling 223 miles. The scorching summer sun was about to relent for the day. Fatigue was enveloping my twenty-three-year-old body. And there she was, the reigning record holder in the women's solo division, preparing to depart the ramp in the lead. With a race that spans hundreds of miles, it is common to go hours without encountering a competitor. I could have been thrilled at my opportunity to compete against the best. However, I was agitated and reluctant. Why couldn't she be comfortably ahead of me? Just enough for me to justify continuing with a reserved but steady effort.

But here was the challenge to step up my effort. That was the last thing I wanted to do. I wanted to crawl out of my boat and sleep for twelve hours straight. In that moment, I began to understand what resilience means to me and how to cultivate it.

She had dominated the division the year before and was highly decorated as a female solo paddling racer in other racing circuits. When we saw one another, mutual dread was apparent—not at each other, but in this pivotal situation. This meant battling to the muddy, blistered end and the insanity that comes with it. The other option was to hang back, self-relegating to complacency. Being in the lead puts a target on your back. The finish line was a long way off, so that target would be there for a long time. There were easily fifteen hours of racing left, predominantly at night. Even if the current record holder fell back, other competitors were gunning for the lead.

Not only is it tough to perform at a high level, but it's difficult to even stay in the race at all. Being in the front of the pack means competing to the point of nerve numbness in body parts like your butt, toes, and fingers. There are also swollen joints, weathered skin, and minimal-to-no sleep for forty-eight hours or more. This was indeed an ultramarathon race, a test of fortitude and perseverance. This was not a wellness retreat with sunrise yoga. This was aching muscles, condensed food, unusual urination methods, and hallucinations all in the name of competition and comradery through self-induced struggle.

This fellow racer had years of racing experience. And there I was, still a novice, fried by the sun for the last two days. My extremities had lost all dexterity. Hello nubby hands. My ground crew mom was hustling to restock my water and food from the ramp. What lay ahead of me was to paddle my lightweight racing canoe through the moonlit river, trying to decipher the channel while dodging buoys, rock dikes, or warped river bends that looked like an M.C. Escher drawing. There would be temptations to take breaks, grab a nap, even quit. I would have to dig deep and stay the course.

My ground crew mom had observed my competitor's fatigue at the boat ramp and was hopeful that this might be the chance to take the lead. However, my mental reserves were taxed. My body was drained. All I wanted was to peacefully paddle as I repeated meditative mantras (or more likely earworm song lyrics) on loop in my head. Sprinting the last river stretch was unfathomable. "Kate," she reinforced, "You. Have. Stamina." This snapped me back to the task at hand. And the task was precisely this: to take the lead, I would need to paddle nonstop through the night.

I left the checkpoint and eventually gained on my competitor. Stroke for stroke, our gap was closing. Soon we were side by side. "What's up, Katie Jo?" she greeted. Between our paralleled grit, we were exhausted enough to let competitive facades subside. We made small river talk, commiserating briefly. The decision to pull ahead was wrought with doubt. I would be admitting that, yes, I have the audacity to go for this. What if I could not sustain the lead or, worse, bonked entirely? There are multiple micro-decisions about when and how to refuel on a quick protein bar or how to use the bathroom strategically to maintain a lead. Flipping my boat could easily cost me a position or two in the rankings.

Alas, I pulled ahead as night fell. There was still a solid 100 miles left in the race. Yes, you read that right. I was not excited to be narrowly in the divisional lead; I was mostly apoplectic. Keeping my head in the right space was a constant effort. "Keep it together, Katie. You can sleep when you finish." There were still other boat ramps remaining, if needed. Maybe just a quick little, teeny-tiny nap? My focus was so shattered that I sometimes forgot what I was doing. Oh yeah . . . paddling. On a river. In a race.

Am I awake? Yes. I'm pretty sure at least. Anxiety seeped into my altered state of mind. However, I was consoled by some wisdom this competitor had shared with me the prior year. We were paddling together briefly during the first night of the race. "Paddling by yourself at night is hard, but that's when you have real solitude."

Back to the current race, another boat's light appeared behind me in the distance at four o'clock in the morning. This was likely to be a boat in another division and not a direct threat, but it could very well be a fellow division competitor. Too risky to hold back only to be passed. I would have to keep up the hustle or potentially forfeit the lead. "Hold it together, girl. The sun will be up soon."

Daybreak brought clarity, both figuratively and literally. My pace put me at the finish line midmorning. It was way too soon to assume I was in the clear. The finish line was still 30 miles away. The crisp morning would soon give way to summer heat. I would have to sustain what was becoming unsustainable. My hands were decrepit, and I smelled like a gnarly football locker room. The final bridge just upstream of the finish line came into view, blurred by the tears that came to my eyes. My boat touched the finish line at ten o'clock in the morning. My name was etched as the first place in the women's solo division, with a new division record.

At fifteen years old, I wanted to be a lifeguard. The prerequisite swimming test included retrieving a ten-pound brick from the bottom of the pool and kicking back to the pool edge with the brick on my chest. I was not able to keep my head above water with the brick on my chest, and I failed. I was heartbroken. Eventually, I came to see the failed brick retrieval as a low point upon which to build. Flash forward to adulthood, I trudged up a beach after swimming 2.4 miles in the ocean as part of an Ironman triathlon. This was the most ambitious swimming endeavor I had attempted. The path from the beach to the bike corral was lined with bricks—a symbol for the progress I had made since my teenage lifeguard ambitions.

Perhaps this is why endurance racing appeals to me. It is my opportunity to practice resilience. It is raw, invigorating, punishing, and soul stirring. It rips the protective covering from my nerve endings and presses my existence against harsh stimuli. And in doing so leaves indelible marks that I often revisit for inspiration. In her 2016 book *The Upside of Stress*, Kelly McGonigal says, "Even in circumstances of great suffering, human beings have a natural capacity to find hope, exert choice, and make meaning. This is why in our own lives, the most common effects of stress include strength, growth, and resilience."

Endurance racing has taught me that the opportunities to be resilient come when I am feeling exhausted, unsure, or down. But that is precisely the environment for self-improvement. I often recall the paddling race during that 2008 summer. Even when feeling defeated, I picked up my paddle and shoved off from the boat ramp into the river current and into the night. Facing the long night ahead, daybreak illuminated a new version of myself.

Kate (Pfefferkorn) Mansker graduated from the University of Missouri–Columbia with a degree in chemical engineering. She owns Pfefferkorn Engineering & Environmental, a family-owned firm she owns with her brother. Kate is married to Scott, the founder of the MR340 canoe and kayak race. She has a son, a stepson, and a stepdaughter.

Prior to starting a family and a business, Kate spent her free time training for and participating in triathlons, marathons, and paddling races after running her first marathon at age twenty-one. Kate was also in the 2012 Guinness Book of World Records for having paddled the farthest distance in twenty-four hours on moving water by a female.

While in college, Kate started the student chapter of Engineers Without Borders at the University of Missouri–Columbia. During this time, she participated in a geotechnical stabilization project in a rural Bolivian village in the Andes Mountains.

Weng Horak

Resilience for Rescues

I could probably write a book about my life. I was born in San Juan, Batangas, Philippines, to parents with very little material wealth. They did, however, have the foresight to allow me to be raised by a prominent local family who adopted me as their own child. They taught me the importance of helping people less fortunate than us and the necessity of getting a good education, and they instilled in me the desire to achieve my goals in life.

I grew up having two families: my biological family and my adopted family. My adopted family raised me from the age of eight months. I'd say the people who raised me were considered influential and well-to-do by Philippine standards, but they also understood their responsibility to their workers, who lived rent-free on their agricultural lands and raised the crops and tended to the livestock with their families in exchange for an equal share of the harvest. I love them all dearly, and I'm very close to everyone in my extended family.

My adopted family was very "old school," and I was raised to dutifully respect my elders. However, I was also raised to speak my mind, to always do the right thing, and to be considerate of other people's feelings and opinions. I especially remember Christmas during my childhood because my family would put together gift packs that we'd hand out to anyone who knocked on our front door. Friends, neighbors, workers, and even total strangers—we'd gladly give them gifts to put smiles on their faces, even if just for a day. When we had our holiday meals, our door was always open for all who were hungry. All were welcome, and we'd even make sure to send them home with plastic bags filled with food for their families. My adoptive parents, who are now deceased, never turned away another person in need, and I like to think that I'm the person I am today because of the life lessons I learned from them.

After graduating high school at age sixteen, my family sent me to a private Catholic college in Manila (population of nine million, then). I graduated in four years with a BS in Accountancy and a master's degree in Business Administration, eventually becoming a certified public accountant and internal auditor. I was hired by United Parcel Service, where at the age of twenty-four I found myself managing a staff of twenty-five people in four different departments. Every morning I would wake up at five a.m. and walk to the bus stop to catch a bus into the heart of the city, which took hours because of the traffic. And since I had siblings who needed help with their school tuition, I'd often work until eleven p.m. or midnight so I could get overtime pay. I'd ride the bus home, fall asleep, and wake up early the next day to do it again. It was hard, especially once I became pregnant with my first child. There were complications with my pregnancy, yet no matter how sick or exhausted I felt, I knew I had to persevere and continue pushing myself for the sake of my and my family's futures. After eight years at UPS, I moved on to other positions in different companies to further my career, until I landed my dream position as a group CFO for a venture capital firm based in London. There I led the finance team responsible for operating Airbus A320 training schools at the former Clark Air Base in the Philippines, as well as in Sharjah, Dubai, and Abu Dhabi in the United Arab Emirates.

In 2008, I married my American fiancé, David, who lived in the Philippines then, and we moved to his hometown of St. Louis, Missouri. The United States economy and job market were in recession at the time, so I had difficulty finding a job. I put in job applications everywhere—including stocking grocery store shelves—but had no luck at all. It was a frustrating and sobering experience not being able to find any job after having been a CFO months earlier. Again, I didn't give up, and after a year I finally secured a position as CFO of a small construction firm, where I spent the next three years. As a small company, we struggled greatly trying to compete against larger, more established firms. Every week I'd have to figure out how to pay our bills and pay our workers. On many Friday mornings you could find me at our general contractor's office practically begging them to release our funds ASAP knowing that the wives of our workers would be at our office Friday afternoon to pick up their husbands' checks. I thought about giving up that job soon after being hired, due to the emotional and mental challenges I faced weekly, but that's not the kind of person I am. My boss gave me a chance when no one else would, so I stuck with it until she eventually moved to Florida.

I then entered the animal rescue world as CFO of a local animal nonprofit in St. Louis, where I remained for the next nine years. During that time my eyes were opened to the horrors of animal abuse and neglect, and I swore I would be part of the solution to that problem not just locally but also nationally. This led to me starting my own nonprofit organization, CARE STL.

In October 2018, the City of St. Louis Department of Health issued a Public Request for Proposal to partner with a nonprofit organization to operate their Animal Care and Control (ACC) shelter. Shocked to discover that nearly 45 percent of the animals that ended up at City ACC were eventually euthanized for lack of space and lack of adopters, I felt it was my moral responsibility to use my fifteen-plus years of corporate and financial experience, as well as my seven years of animal rescue/shelter experience, to try to save those 45 percent of animals who were being euthanized. So I spent five or six hours every night after work, for three months, crafting a proposal to the Department of Health and putting together a team of experienced people who would eventually become CARE STL.

Now, nearly five years later, we struggle every day to come up with solutions to the problems we face, trying to house and care for all the animals we have and continue to get on a daily basis. We are always filled to capacity, and beyond. Yet as an open intake, no-kill shelter (with a lifesaving rate of 99 percent), we rarely turn away any animal in need. Every day we reach out in multiple ways to the community to help us by adopting or fostering a dog or cat, or by at least giving an animal twenty-four to forty-eight hours of "straycation" away from the shelter. This is a 365 day per year undertaking, and it takes a great deal of perseverance, creativity, and adaptability on our part to keep moving forward no matter how large this task sometimes seems.

Another main struggle is always the budget. Saving the lives of more than 3,000 animals a year—feeding them, cleaning up after them, providing physical exercise and socialization, and providing them with proper medical care, etc.—requires at least $1.2 million annually, but the City budget is only $677K. So a critical part of our operation is raising additional funds for the other half of our operating expenses. For us to maintain a 99 percent save rate, we must raise a lot of money to cover these costs. Making payroll, as well as paying our veterinary bills, is often difficult. I like to say I knock on people's hearts for them to donate so we can continue our work for these animals. I wear numerous hats in my organization because we can't afford to hire more people. I clean kennels in the morning and attend meetings in the afternoon, all the while thinking of new ways to increase funding so we can keep the shelter open, and I do it seven days a week. When you have your own business, you put your entire life into it, and I believe that's what I've done with CARE STL.

I've always been an outgoing person, even as a child, climbing on rooftops and trees to play games with my friends while singing "How Much Is That Doggie in the Window?" at the top of my lungs. My love for my childhood pets and the passion for helping others that I learned from my adopted family have enabled me to create CARE STL. I've used a lifetime of personal and career experiences to find my true calling: serving the community by helping the downtrodden, voiceless animals of St. Louis. We've saved thousands of animals' lives so far, and we intend to save thousands more as we continue to grow and become even more of a fixture in our city.

Weng Horak is the CEO and Founder of the Center for Animal Rescue and Enrichment of St. Louis—CARE STL, a Black, Indigenous, and People of Color (BIPOC) led organization. Weng founded the organization to create a supportive community rooted in collaboration, compassion, and caring for people and animals. She works collaboratively with the City of St. Louis Department of Health to enforce the city laws relevant to animal care and control. Weng embraces the No-Kill Model and follows the guiding principles of no-kill shelters.

Weng is a forward-thinking, results-oriented, hands-on leader with more than twenty-four years of progressive work experience in finance, accounting, HR, and operations. In 2020, Weng was recognized for her innovative solution-oriented work and featured in *People* Magazine, *USA Today*, and on Access Hollywood, NBC, and KSDK's *Making a Difference* segment of Channel 5 News. Weng was recently named 2022 Titan 100—a program recognizing St. Louis's Top 100 CEO & C-level executives.

Susan Stiers

There Are No Rules

Early in my career, I worked for a small manufacturing company in a small town in the middle of the USA. The business made a product that was in the mature phase of its life cycle, meaning the product had been around a long time and there was a lot of competition that kept prices low. In addition, the same product was being mass-produced overseas for a much lower price. No matter what we did, we couldn't get our costs down enough to be competitive with import prices.

As a young manager, I dreamed of buying the company one day and running it myself. I plotted ways to expand our capability, economize to lower expenses, and give back to our community. Several times I took my ideas to the owner, who was too busy bailing water out of his sinking ship to look ahead and make a plan. I looked around at my coworkers and worried about how they would pay for groceries or rent when the company failed. It was tough to watch as the business slid down into what turned out to be a hard landing. The owner eventually closed the company after deciding his best bet was to get a good price for the real estate. The business closure was hard. It was not only the loss of possibly becoming the owner and watching my coworker friends now become unemployed; it was also the loss of my own job and livelihood, which supported my family.

Shortly after the business closed, one of our long-time customers (who I had become friends with over the years) called me at home. He wanted to know if I could tell him where to find products now that our company would no longer be supplying him. A light bulb went off, and without thinking it through, I said, "I can supply that for you. I'm starting my own business and carrying the same type of products." He said, "Great, where do I send my PO?" And the rest is history. That was almost twenty years ago.

I financed the start-up of my business with the profit from that first order. I quickly set up an LLC and a small business bank account. I called the competition of my former employer and asked to be set up as a wholesale account. I bought a fax machine and set up an email address so that I could start accepting purchase orders. I put the word out to my former customers and started getting orders. I set up a desk in the corner of my bedroom and designed my own website. I ran my business in the evening and on weekends while I worked full time and took care of my home and family. During this time, I went to school at night to finish my bachelor's degree and later earned an MBA. It wasn't perfect, and it wasn't always easy, but I finally owned my own company. Little did I know in the beginning, but this business would provide extra income that helped send all three of my children through college. I'm the proudest of this part of the story. Two of my children went on to earn doctorates, and all three are successful and, most importantly, happy in their careers.

I could have given up on my dream of being a business owner when my employer closed the company. I could have taken it personally that, as a manager, I should have been able to help turn the business around. But every race you are brave enough to run will come to an end. Some in a victory, some in a defeat. And the defeat you suffer today does not mean that a win will never happen again.

Resilience can be defined as the ability to withstand adversity, adapt to the situation, and bounce back from the tough things that happen to us in life. In the world of work, resilience is also an important factor to build into your team environment. The question is, "How do we exercise and strengthen our resilience muscles in ourselves?"

If you are looking for ways to build your resilient strength, think back to when you pushed through and felt strong when you came out of a tough time. If you can remember that feeling of strength and calm, you can remind yourself that you will get through whatever current troubles are facing you as well. Another way to become more resilient is to proactively address issues before they become problems. Figure out what needs to be done and plan to take steps that will get you there. Give yourself grace as you work toward your goal. Consider journaling as a tool to help guide you—as well as a way to look back—the next time you see trouble ahead. When you are facing adversity, take good care of yourself. Your feelings are valid, whatever they are, and talking about them may help. Sleeping well, eating well, and continuing to exercise are important to your well-being when you are working through a tough time.

Although it can be tempting, curling up in a ball or pulling the covers over your head won't solve any problems. They will still be waiting there to be dealt with when you emerge. I know a person who rarely leaves her home or the small town where she lives. Either consciously or subconsciously she made the decision to stay where she felt safest. I don't know what trauma could have happened to her to convince her to shrink her world to such a manageable little size. But that sense of safety she thinks she has created is false. The world is the size it is, and keeping yourself out of the way in a corner to make it more easily digestible doesn't mean that bad things will never happen to you. A small life with no deviation may keep you safe from airplane crashes and tsunamis, but when you reach the end, it will be just a small life, and you won't get a do-over. Trips with family you missed, new foods not tried, long walks not taken, and conversations never spoken are what you'll have given up in that trade-off. That's not a life. Find the resilience in yourself that allows you to go out into the world and do the things that make your life rich and full. Feel joy in the time you spend at work, with your family, and with friends. Maybe not every day, but most days.

As a Kansas City Chiefs fan, when I'm watching a game, I think about the resilience it takes for a quarterback to keep firing the ball down the field. Any throw could be picked off by the other team and end in an interception. Every play can end in a physical injury, potentially serious enough to end a career. What makes the quarterback keep coming back on the field game after game? It can't just be the paycheck; he probably already has enough money for the rest of his life. It can't just be the cheers of the crowd, because he already knows that on a bad day they will boo instead of cheer. But he also knows that every time he takes the field is an opportunity to achieve greatness. Another chance to become a legend and put his name in record books that will live on long after he is gone. It's the chance to be great that makes him suit up and run onto the field, even on the days when it's a hundred degrees or twenty degrees, or when he has a parent in the hospital or a sick child at home. He knows that greatness won't happen if he stays in the locker room. That's the way resilient people approach life, knowing each new day is an opportunity for something awesome to happen.

I hope that your takeaway from my story is to think outside your own box. My choice was to get married and have my children early. I went back to school to finish my degree later, not earning my MBA until I was fifty. Here's the thing: There are no rules. There is no one coming to check to make sure you are doing things in the right order. There are many, many, many paths to success. Mine might not be right for you, and yours might not be right for me, but we will both get there. After all, that is what being resilient is all about.

Susan Stiers is a serial entrepreneur with a love of growing small businesses. Her best quality is taking true joy in seeing others succeed, especially her fellow women. Her worst quality is not being able to say no, which has landed her more volunteer roles than she can count.

By day she's a human resources director. But in her spare time, she owns Nasus Supply LLC—a certified female-owned wholesale distributor—and Nasus Management LLC, a property management business for guest houses in the tourism town of Hermann, Missouri. She also partners with friends in residential and commercial real estate development and looks for ways to grow the town and state economies.

Susan's proudest accomplishment is her family. She feels lucky to watch her children's journeys as they make their own families. They are all her pride and joy. She could, however, use a puppy if anyone has a spare pandemic goldendoodle.

Amy Yan

Authors of Our Lives

For twenty-three years I struggled mentally and physically. I woke up every day feeling depressed and unmotivated. I felt overwhelmed with the amount of work and expectations that others had placed on me. I was in a place of negativity and drowning in my own sorrows. I was stuck in a dark place in my life where I missed so much time with my three children. I missed school events, I missed sports activities, I missed just being in their lives. I had no idea what work-life balance meant and how not having it would affect my life. The negative feelings I had for so long drained me. I didn't feel like I was me.

At times I felt alone and didn't really have anyone to speak to about my problems. I felt that going to my husband about my feelings would dump my problems on him. I was struggling to find peace, joy, and happiness within my surroundings and within myself. I thought where I was in life was where I had to be, and I had no other choice but to stay in that dark place. Little did I know I was on my way to learning how strong and resilient I truly am.

I wasn't sure how to improve the course of my life because I had always been scared to make changes. I never strayed away from doing anything that wasn't familiar. Someone once told me that doing the same thing over and over again, thinking you will have a different result, is called insanity. That's what I was doing. I was making myself insane thinking that I could change how I felt, but I never changed anything else I was doing, so my complacency held me in the same place. Change is what I needed to overcome the bad place I was at in life. I just didn't know how or what I needed to change to make that happen.

I struggled for a long time to find the answers I needed. I spoke to many other women who were going through hard times in their lives to learn how they overcame it. They all pretty much told me the same thing: If I wanted something to change in my life, then I was the only person who could do it.

During the pandemic I realized I had an opportunity to change my life. We were forced to stay indoors with our family, and I realized everything I was missing in life. My kids and my husband were all I needed to stay positive, to be happy, and to find the peace I was missing. It was then when I knew that I am the only person who can change what happens next. This was the moment my resilience kicked in.

From that moment, I decided to start my own business. I wanted to balance my work with my personal life so that I could be more involved with my family. Having my own business meant I would be able to work when I wanted and still be there for my family. In 2021, I started my business, and this day I couldn't be happier with the decision I made.

I have chosen a path that has helped me find peace, joy, and happiness within myself. I feel more refreshed with my life. I have more gratitude for everything that surrounds me. I wake up feeling more motivated to start my day and more positive than ever. Who would have thought that I had the capability to be able to change my life, just as other women before me have done?

I learned that my life and all the things that happen in it are caused by my decisions. Had I chosen to stay in that negativity and unhappiness,

I would still be in a bad place. I chose to be resilient and rise above it. I chose to write the next chapters in my life, and I grew so much stronger. I now knew that my life could be whatever I wanted it to be. I decide what's in my next chapter of life because I am the author of my own life. We are all the authors of our own lives. What we do determines what lies ahead.

If you are feeling stuck in a dark place like I was, here is my advice for you. You can stay in a place of negativity, or you can rise above it. You can drown yourself in work, or you can create a better work-life balance. You can be in a place of depression, or you can look for all the good in life. You can do whatever you want to do, feel however you want to feel, and be whatever you want to be by having faith in knowing that it is you who can make that change. No one else can change your life but you.

No one can tell you how to live your life. You are the only person who can make the necessary changes to be where you want to be. If you want to live a happier, less stressful life, then you can do it. Believing in yourself is where you will find the strength to change. When you realize you are the author of your future, your whole mindset will change.

As your mindset changes, you will become more aware that what you're going through today is not what you have to endure. You become stronger in knowing that your future relies on you. You have the strength and the resources within yourself to come out on top. You have everything you need within yourself to make changes in your life for the better.

Resilience to me means being able to break through any barriers you have in life—overcoming obstacles that appear to be set in stone and finding the strength to overcome them. Resilience is rising above any thing that may bring you down. It is the force within you to keep going no matter what. We all have resilience embedded in us already. Once you find it you can be the author of your own life and start living the life of your dreams.

Born in Belleville, Illinois, in 1981, Amy faced many challenges being socially and economically disadvantaged. With hard work and determination, she was able to overcome any obstacle. Amy was hired on, full time, by a local IT company where she spent twenty-three years of her employment. She started as a secretary and quickly worked her way up to Sales and Service Consultant.

Being a minority woman in a male-dominated industry didn't stop her from being successful and reaching her goals. In 2021, Amy founded C Three Business Consultants. Her success today proves that nothing can stop you from living the American dream.

Derlene Hirtz

The Calming of My Perfect Storm

"What the hell do you mean 'what are my dreams'?"

That was my response the day my journey back to self was about to begin. When asked that question, I couldn't even fathom having dreams. I was just surviving in life, trying to get through the day. I spent hours every day asking myself, "Why do I feel like this (a failure, a fraud, an imposter)? What's wrong with me? Why can't I ever feel happy?"

Around that same time, my soldier son announced he was going to Afghanistan for the first time. He was a Ranger and knew he would be directly in harm's way. It became obvious that I had no tools to deal with the crippling fear of what could happen (death or, even worse, torture). It was more than this momma's heart could bear. This created the perfect storm that completely paralyzed every area of my life.

If I was going to survive this storm, I knew it would only happen if I found some tools to help me through this dark period. I looked at myself in the mirror and got completely honest with myself. I asked (myself), "Do you truly want more tools, or are you going to live your life so disempowered?" That woman staring me back in the mirror answered a definite, "*Yes*, more tools!" I picked up the phone and called a life/business coach who I had been introduced to earlier. That phone call changed my life.

This is why the majority of people remain stuck. They say "no" for a lot of reasons, and every one of them is rooted in fear. "What if these tools don't work, what then?" "I've tried things in the past, they didn't work." "At least I know what happens tomorrow if I stay here," and so on. It's a safe place to dwell, however unhappy it is.

That phone call will always stick with me. That was the day I looked in the mirror and saw an unhappy, sad, fearful woman staring back at me. I hardly recognized her, and yet she was very familiar. She was full of self-doubt, lacking self-worth, no confidence, and listening constantly to that negative mind chatter that I call the "Itty-Bitty Shitty Committee" that kept playing in her mind. And she just wanted to quit life.

I began working with that coach. One day I asked her what it was that helped me shift my thinking so fast, and she told me it was Neuro-Linguistic Programming. NLP is the science and study of success and how to use the brain to get the results you want in all areas of life. I became intrigued, took vacation from work, and traveled to California several times so that I could learn what it was I didn't know. The training did not disappoint!

I soon realized that I was working in a toxic environment. And it had taken its toll. I know what you feed grows and what you starve dies, and I had been ingesting toxins for a while. Bottom line, I was compromising my values and it was the biggest conflict of all. I just didn't know it at the time.

Looking back, I see that time as a great opportunity to gain resilience—a life skill that we acquire over time and experience. It is not a crisis-only situation. It's about stepping up to the challenge and taking advantage of the opportunities that offer learnings which make us wiser, stronger, and more skilled. It is standing up, looking fear in the face, and facing the unknown.

Resilience means at some point we get to make choices that either will (or will not) result in taking responsibility for our actions, thoughts, beliefs, failures, and successes. The moment we decide to take responsibility is *the* moment we become empowered.

At fifty-two years old, when all my friends were retiring, staying at home with their grandchildren, and playing pickleball, I made a life-changing decision to become an entrepreneur. I wanted to know what it felt like. Well, I certainly know now!

By the time I was out of eighth grade, I had gone to five different schools. I understood how to make new friends, I understood that friends just passed through my life, and I knew that to make new friends, I had to be one. Resilience lesson #1.

When I told my father at fifty-two years of age that I was going to become an entrepreneur and a business owner, he said, "I'm really glad you have a roof over your head." As a matter of fact, he said that to me three times during a ten-minute conversation. At first, I was hurt, and that little five-year-old Derlene wanted to gather up those hurt feelings and hide. Resilience lesson #33.

Instead, I embraced my newly found understanding that my father's map of reality was far different than mine. I understand that people do the best they can with the tools they have. It was very easy for me to understand my father because I knew what he said was out of love. He did not understand my world.

Accepting that we all do the best we can with the tools we have is one of the greatest gifts. It is also what I call a "forgiveness clause." All the years of berating myself resulted in some seriously negative self-talk. Once I truly embraced that I did the best I could with the resources I had, it became easy to shift my mindset. It was freeing! Resilience lesson #102.

When I began my company, You Empowered Services, I thought it would be *easy*. You know, hang a sign that says "Open for Business," go to a few networking meetings, and *boom*! Success!

It's more like the dark night of the soul. The darkest night came for me when I texted my coach with the news that I had only four people attending a workshop, zero people coming for support, and I sucked at selling. It was the first, and only, time I thought to myself, "I can't do this."

That little Pity Party lasted about twelve hours. Quite an improvement from years past when they would last for weeks at a time! Funny thing about pity parties: no one ever comes. It is usually a party for one.

This time, instead of getting stuck in the "why" of it all, I reminded myself that I was educated more than most in my mindset. I did, in fact, have the tools and it was time to put them to work. Resilience lesson #300-ish.

Within two days, I signed three new clients/students and have been in go-go mode ever since. Resilience at its best.

My greatest lesson to date is knowing that people show up in our life at the perfect time. Some we know as friends, some as foes, some we don't know at all. Make no mistake, they are there to mirror for us so we can continue to evolve. If we fail to learn, the lesson shows up again and again. Until eventually a two-by-four plank shows up and we do or die (metaphorically). My two-by-four was my former boss. Oh, I had opportunities prior to seeing the lessons that constantly compromised my values; I just chose to ignore them.

T.D. Jakes, a businessman and preacher, says that we can never really appreciate the destination if we do not experience the struggles along the way. It is so true. The journey is what builds our resilience. If all I had to do was hang a sign that read "Open for Business," I could never be the success I am today. It is the struggles, the sleepless nights, the tears, the prayers, even the pleading, that defines my success. Resilience lesson 473 … and counting.

Derlene Hirtz helps high-achieving entrepreneurs, business owners, and sales professionals who are ready to level up their success, to include business, relationships, and finances. Her clients come to her when they have hit a wall and realize they have more potential and cannot reach it on their own.

Derlene Hirtz is the Chief Empowerment Officer (CEO) at You Empowered Services. She is a Transformational Success Coach, Neuro-Linguistic Programming (NLP) trainer, and professional speaker. Derlene is the author of the bestseller *Journey of Intention*.

Derlene is an expert in helping transform lives to unstoppable success. She brings her intensive NLP training, years as an educator, director of education, trainer, and transformational coach to help others gain a positive attitude, lasting motivation, increase sales, and overall more happiness and fulfillment in life and business.

Her greatest love is that of Gigi to four grandchildren, and as wife, mom, daughter, and friend.

Ree Hamlin

Don't Just Park—Parallel Park!

The day before my dad left for Vietnam the second time, he took me to get my driver's license and I flunked! Passing my driver's test would have meant that I could help my mom with my five sisters and brothers while my dad was gone. It was also my chance to show my dad that I could pass the test before he left. So much for that thought! I did eventually pass and was able to help my mom that year, but that disappointing moment in time has never left me. Did I learn something from it? Yes, of course! I flunked because I couldn't parallel park (and I still can't). Is that the end of the story? A resounding no! I may not have learned how to parallel park, but I did learn that you don't have to be an expert at everything you do to accomplish your goals.

As a wife, stepmom, gramma, daughter, sister, aunt, godmother, friend, and business team leader, I am blessed with many people in my life. Every person in our lives is trying to pass their driver's license test. My dad didn't make me feel bad about not passing my test. He reminded me that I needed to practice my parallel parking and that I had a responsibility to my family. Responsibilities can bring you down or make you stronger. What you do with them is up to you. When I had the opportunity to marry an amazing man with three young children, I didn't hesitate, but I had a lot to learn. Most importantly I needed to learn that my expectations as a single person without children didn't always equate to the lives and paths of my new family. They taught me unconditional love without expectations. The paths they have taken in life are all different, but somehow, they manage to support each other and maintain the closest bond of a family that I have ever seen. The support of my husband and family makes it possible for me to continue to grow and learn every day. I am so lucky to have been a part of this family for the last twenty-nine years!

Growing up as a female in the 50's, 60's and 70's gave me the opportunity to achieve many firsts. In the 70's I was one of the first non-pharmacists and female assistant managers for Walgreens – at that time only 1% of the managers at Walgreens were non pharmacists and/or female. I was the first female non pharmacist manager for a small chain of drug stores in St. Louis in the 80's. I spent most of my career in the pharmacy industry. Most of the time I was the only female or the first female at the table. Through those firsts I was given the opportunity to help and mentor other women to leadership roles at Fortune 500 companies. Ironically, my mentors were typically males who had accomplished great things in their careers and were willing to be my mentor and help me and other women advance our careers—I am very grateful to all of them. I retired from my leadership role as a Director of Sales for Cardinal Health in 2018. My team at Cardinal Health was incredible and thrived on diverse thought and leadership. After retirement from Cardinal Health, I found an opportunity to publish community magazines. I founded and started the first Best Version Media community magazine in Webster Groves in 2020. I love my "encore" career, publishing magazines and helping businesses and business owners in the local St. Louis area accomplish their dreams of growing their businesses.

I am fortunate to be able to say that I grew up in a family with a long line of women who didn't let the fact that they were women stop them from striving for their dreams. My mom, who is eight-nine years old recently, told me that she wants to get an iWatch. Most seniors her age don't even know how to use a computer. My mom doesn't see age as a roadblock; she just finds new routes and continues to inspire and amaze me.

When we were growing up, my dad was a Marine officer. My mom was a Marine wife. I always say she was the colonel in the family. She had to be because my dad was away from home and out of the country or at war three different times for fifteen months by the time I was eighteen. During the time my dad was gone, my mom raised six children. The truth of the matter is I never saw my mom in bed except for when she had a baby or once a year when she got sick. She was up before we were in the morning and after at night, and she made our clothes and practiced the piano. In later years, she got a degree, worked for the Marines/Navy and Army. My favorite job of hers was when she helped create and purchase the advertising for the Army. Once a month Mom went to New York City and worked with major ad agencies.

My dad was my mom's biggest fan and supporter. Right before the pandemic, my mom was given an award as one of the top literacy tutors in the state of Illinois. At eight-nine, my mom still teaches literacy to at least three different students a week on Zoom. She is also a grandma and great-grandma and has great relationships with each and every one of them.

She has always been, and continues to be, a great example of what "resilience" means. Resilience is defined as the capacity to recover quickly from difficulties. The ability to spring back into shape. When I was young, I wanted to be an astronaut. The first woman to orbit the Earth was Valentina Tereshkova on the Soviet Vostok 6. The first woman from the United States to go to space was Sally Ride on the Space Shuttle Challenger on June 18, 1983. John Glenn was a role model for me. I have read his autobiography twice. Remember the book and movie *Hidden Figures*? John Glenn wouldn't have made it to space without the help of those amazing women behind the scenes. Today women are anything that they want to be. That does not mean it is easy, but with determination and support from others who have had been "the firsts," it is possible for women to achieve their dreams. I recently heard someone talking about their mentors and role models. The thing I took away from it was that everyone around you at every moment can be a mentor if you are willing to open your heart to the gifts of differences, enlightenment, and experiences each person brings. We are constantly looking for people who have achieved amazing things to be our mentors. It is easy for us to not see what is in front of us and to not accept the gifts we are given. Resilience teaches us to look backward and forward and learn from everyone and every experience we have.

Does not passing my driver's license test with my dad still bother me today? To be honest, yes, but what a gift it was. All of my life I wanted to make my dad and mom happy. Not passing my driver's license test the day before my dad left for Vietnam was just another way I learned to strive to be the best at everything I do and to see and accept the gifts that each first gives me. I wish you many firsts and the ability to accept the gifts that are given to you every day!

I dedicate this chapter to my younger sister Paula Hamlin. Paula always wanted to write a book but left us before she could finish it seventeen years ago. Paula was my mentor and inspiration and will always be one of the most important people in my life.

Ree Hamlin is a visionary leader and a community-oriented entrepreneur. She is founder and CEO of *Neighbors of Webster Groves*, a Best Version Media publication. Ree's goal is to bring people together by helping small, medium, and large businesses grow through micro-targeted community marketing.

Prior to setting up her own marketing business, Ree held sales leadership positions in the Independent Sales Force of Cardinal Health and two other key pharmaceutical wholesale companies. Ree holds a Bachelor of Arts degree in Management and Communications with a minor in Human Resources from Concordia University.

On the personal side, Ree is married to Tom Lewis, who is retired from Ameren Electric where he was a Unit Operating Engineer. Ree and Tom have three grown children who are all married. They have six grandchildren, and you can almost always find them at sports or school activities supporting them.

Dr. Jodi Jordan

My Path to Finding Joy

Finding joy means so much more than just getting happy. It is about recognizing your unique and individual giftedness and celebrating every occasion. The journey to finding joy began after my displacement from employment in 2020. My job loss is no longer important, but the lessons I learned are life-giving. This new phase in my life is synonymous with grace, moving forward, and new purpose.

For more than thirty years, I served as an educator, a teacher, administrator, school founder, advisor, and consultant. I have prided myself on being a hard worker, responsible, and committed. I was successful in my work, but it always felt like an uphill battle. I sought validation from individuals who did not recognize my potential. I often thought about leaving the position, but I continued to fight because I could do the work. I was committed to the staff and families whom I was serving, regardless of how my supervisors treated me. I believed that one day, the right leader would come along and "see" me. I thought I was happy enough. I had a job with a decent salary. I had purpose. I was needed. But I had no joy. Displacement helped me find the courage I needed to review my life and to begin the journey to find joy.

Happiness is different than joy. Happiness is merely an emotion. Joy is like fruit that grows and develops inside of you. It spreads into all the areas of your life. It fills up the empty spaces and encompasses goals of purpose, ability, living authentically, owning one's truth, and pursuing one's destiny.

So how does one find joy? As I journeyed down this path, I began to assess my skills and my talents, and to question, "Who is Jodi?" This honest assessment identified both strengths and deficits. More importantly, I discovered my *internal adequacy*. This is a term I coined in my dissertation research about African American women in doctoral programs. The research states that African American women pursuing doctoral studies persist largely due to feelings of internal adequacy. They faced overcoming various challenges and barriers to completion by developing coping mechanisms, such as positive self-talk and a refusal to abandon the process. They persisted because they believed they could. Internal adequacy is the sum of a person's belief in themselves and what they can achieve—their strength, resilience, and their internal support. It speaks to what is already inside of a person, and how who they are is beneficial and adequate for pursuing and possessing joy.

Self-reflection is an important part of resilience and joy. Understanding our motivations plays an important role in how we see ourselves. We see ourselves based on how we are perceived by others and the value they assign to us. When I looked in the mirror, I did not recognize myself. I saw a woman who was tired, broken, and lacking confidence. My reflection revealed how I'd neglected my emotional and physical health. My primary focus had been external. I was driven to be a great leader, a good wife and mother, a strong minister/leader at my church, etc., and gave of myself to achieve many goals. A further look at myself revealed heartbreak and how the effects of betrayal and disloyalty had disrupted trust and caused me to withdraw from social relationships and opportunities.

My life had become an ongoing workday, with me being the employee. I fashioned myself as a "Cinderella" type, working and hoping that one day I would be loved and appreciated. This behavior extended to all aspects of my life. On some level I felt unworthy of love, even though plenty of people do in fact love and care for me. They just thought I had it all together. That final look in the mirror displayed the truth of my unhappiness and discontent. My self-esteem was at an all-time low. Instead of being the person who I imagined myself to be, I was the opposite. This honest look at myself was the beginning of my journey to joy.

Following this time of reflection, I took some time to heal. Brokenness displays itself in many ways. For me, it revealed itself as self-doubt, social isolation, and regret. I reviewed my work history. I developed trusted relationships with people who would tell me the truth, and I sought therapy to face things that had damaged me. I removed some people from my circle of friends. I had critical conversations to determine the future of some relationships. Along this path, I was the pathfinder and found that I could determine my direction. Finding joy meant that I had to empower myself and my beliefs about who I was. It was intimidating and I was scared. Yet I wanted to live and not die. I wanted to find joy.

Determined to live differently, I changed the trajectory of my work life. I no longer wanted a one-sided career. I wanted to work for an organization that offered equal opportunity respect and not just a paycheck. Work Culture became part of my job search. Money had never been my biggest issue, but I wanted to earn a certain amount, and in the field of education, salaries are traditionally low. During my time of unemployment, after my displacement, my life was better, even though I did not have much money. The power to live on my own terms and without constant critique and threat brought me joy. I was happy with less money because I gained a different kind of wealth: cultural wealth. Cultural wealth, as defined by Professor Tara J. Yosso, is "an array of knowledge, skills, strengths, and experiences that are learned and shared by people of color and marginalized groups. The values and behaviors that are nurtured through culture work together to create a way of knowing and being." Cultural wealth was a driving force toward gaining joy.

I developed new goals and sought a new career and position that has allowed me to reestablish myself using my skills, intellect, and personality. I projected what I wanted during the interviews. I set expectations. Every position has its responsibilities and requirements. I checked myself and knew that I was adequate and qualified for the job. I decided that I would never allow myself to be mistreated or underappreciated in an employment setting again. In addition to finding a new position, I built new professional networks through civic engagement, new friendships through social involvement, and continued relationship building with current friends and family. I stopped hiding and began to live authentically. I did not wear my pain on my sleeve, but I allowed myself to bleed as I discussed situations with a therapist and trusted friends, to deal with the wounds until they started to heal. I was finding Jodi. I was finding joy unapologetically.

Finding Joy Educational Consultants was founded during this journey. I had spent so many years using my good ideas and my teaching skills to make other organizations better, but I rarely received credit for the wonderful ideas and work. Many of those ideas are still working in places where I am no longer employed. When I considered all I had to offer (internal adequacy), I realized I could provide training and learning opportunities to other audiences. Now organizations pay me to do what I had given away for many years. More than capable, more than qualified, more than adequate, I see now that I am the answer to someone's problem.

I develop solutions and train others to solve problems. My displacement was a blessing in disguise.

Last but not least, on my journey along the path, I acknowledge the role that faith and forgiveness played in my discovery of true joy. I sought forgiveness for things that I had done to hurt people. I also freely forgave those who had offended me. This was sometimes the most difficult part of the process because it is easy to believe that anger and bitterness are beneficial. However, letting go of negative thoughts, memories, and people who have hurt you can lead to a more productive and less stressful life. The release of pain helped me to stop reliving trauma daily. I prayed for those who hurt me. I endeavored to move forward and committed to change in my life. This was emotionally, physically, and spiritually refreshing. I am grateful now for the many experiences that have ultimately led me to finding joy! The journey continues . . .

Dr. Jodi L. Jordan is an accomplished and highly regarded educational leader. Her career spans over three decades in which she has been an educational leader, consultant, university administrator, child advocate, and community servant. Dr. Jordan's expertise includes providing intensive training and technical support to educators. Her passion for education and its importance for all children is reflected in her role as a highly sought facilitator for professional development meetings and seminars in childcare, licensing, curriculum development, and equity and diversity.

An avid learned, Dr. Jordan has earned a BA in Elementary Education and African & African American Studies from Washington University, a MA in Counseling Education from St. Louis University, and an Ed.D. in Educational Administration from St. Louis University.

Currently, Dr. Jordan is a faculty member and the Supervisor at Southern Illinois University at Edwardsville. She is married to Minister LeAndre Jordan, and together they parent six daughters and seven grandchildren.

Tiffany Wright

God Winks

As I take my daily walk down my gravel country road, I am lost in the thought of my journey over the last year. To see the sun come up, watch the leaves change colors, and breathe in cool morning air is something so special. Just like the ebb and flow of the leaves on the trees during my walks in different seasons, my trek in life has been one of growing and resilience and then releasing and letting go. I've learned to quit trying to control everything and let "God Winks" guide me on my new path. To me, "God Winks" are little signs from God that let me know He is with me on my way through life.

A little over a year ago, I quit my corporate job, which I'd held for almost eight years. I put my heart and soul into that job, in every position I held within the company. Right before I left, I was feeling drained, overworked, and guilty because my primary focus was on my career and not on my family. I loved my job, and I loved being busy and constantly trying to do more. But out of the blue, like a ton of bricks, the heaviness of everything finally hit me and I broke down. I reluctantly submitted my resignation and decided to find myself.

During the last couple years of my corporate career, I experienced two miscarriages. One was fairly far along, and though both were difficult, the first one was gut-wrenching. I know people who have had stillborn children, and I know people who have been much further along. I know people who have had children pass away just days after being born. I cannot imagine going through any of those. For me, mine was getting close to fourteen weeks; we were almost able to find out the baby's gender. I saw the baby's heartbeat, and the next week it was gone. I was distraught. I took a day off work and then went right back to it. I went through this a second time, then had a hysterectomy because of several issues.

This was a lot to go through in a short time, but I stayed resilient and decided to focus on work and advance my career. I was promoted from Director of Accounting & HR to the Director of Operations for a real estate investment and management company that my company owned. This was a big jump, and I continued to help with my old position's transition as well. It was an overwhelming amount of change and was hard on my still-healing body and mind. It was busy enough, though, to stay distracted from the internal hurt I was feeling. I pushed through and made several positive changes to the company. I felt so proud to make a difference. Though they were some of the toughest times of my life, I really enjoyed running the company and everything it entailed. I felt like I had finally found my place.

This feeling of being in the right place eventually faded. Once things settled down with the transition at work and things were running more smoothly, I started feeling a nagging sense of unease. Something wasn't quite right. I didn't feel good. I wasn't treating my body well. I felt tired, drained, guilty—all the bad things. What in the world was going on? I had an excellent job, was making great money with lots of perks, had an awesome family and home. The modern American dream, right?

The truth is, I was living someone else's dream. As much as I enjoyed my job, it was taking all of me. I had nothing left *for* me. Nothing left for my family.

Fortunately, as my son and I would call them, a series of "God Winks" occurred.

It started with my husband's job. He worked for his uncle running his poultry farm, and our plan had always been to eventually purchase the farm. I would then stay home and either help at the farm or start a home-based business. It was finally time! The hard work had paid off and we were able to purchase the farm. This was such perfect timing as we also had money saved up and I was ready for a break.

I took the next few months to get the farm set up, and for the first time since I was a kid, took a chunk of time off to find myself. I found out I could draw (kind of!), I learned to make quilts, and I worked in my yard. I will forever be grateful for this time. I talked to God a lot and asked Him to lead me where I could make a difference.

When the time was right, I started a bookkeeping and consulting business and got to do my favorite part of any job I've done in the last decade: overlook financials, organize, and help people see how their company is doing. I love digging in and finding out how a company ticks. I've worked with real estate investors, donut shop owners, farmers, and more; but when it comes down to it, most businesses are pretty much the same. I love seeing people grow their businesses and helping coach them along the way.

God Winks have come along at just the right time, and I've enjoyed working with every client. Several of them were overworked and stressed, and my role in their lives has been more than bookkeeping or consulting, but alleviating some of their stress and letting them feel like someone has their back. People need a good support system, especially in business, because the stress of feeling alone can really eat at your soul. We are made to work together with other people.

I think the hardest part of working from home is the lack of a team environment. I'm a social person, and I've even considered taking another corporate job or going back to my old job because I missed the people. I know, though, the path for me is not going backward. I must stay resilient and move into this new realm of work, where I can spend time with my family, take care of my body, and have time to have a still mind.

When I recently thought about going back to my old job, another God Wink occurred. I was having a rough day, feeling particularly sad about missing my old coworkers. My mind said, "Maybe you should talk to them," but my gut told me no. I did talk to them, but quickly regretted it. Sometimes our feelings of clinging onto the past and what is comfortable drive us to do things we don't mean to do. I felt silly for even thinking about taking another corporate job or going back to my old company. Just because something is more comfortable doesn't mean it is the right path. I felt God tugging at my gut, telling me I had to move on and stop living in the past.

Shortly after feeling I might want to go back into the past, I was asked to write this chapter. I knew it was a God Wink. Just at the right time, something was placed in my lap that I was not expecting. Something new and for the future. I have a goal in life to write a book and had just been thinking about it the night before. On top of the writing, I am getting back to meeting with this group of incredible women leaders and authors, and I look forward to the comradery it will bring. Just when I was feeling isolated, I was asked to return to a group of supportive women. I don't think this is a coincidence. If we allow Him, God will guide us in a better direction than we would have guided ourselves.

My journey has taken a lot of resilience, as I think all our journeys do. Some advice for young women just starting their careers: Take chances and risks to find *your* path. Don't rely on others to tell you what or who you need to be. Be there for people, even if it isn't popular to care. Take care of your family and your health first, then everything else will fall into place. Most importantly, watch for God Winks. They will guide you on your way. When you are truly on the right path, you will know.

Tiffany's passion is seeing small business owners grow their businesses and supporting them on their way. She's the owner of CTR Bookkeeping & Consulting and has more than fifteen years' experience in the business world. Tiffany specializes in helping small businesses optimize their profitability and provides day-to-day accounting services for clients.

Tiffany and her husband, Chase, also own, manage, and run a large poultry farm in rural Missouri.

Tiffany loves being involved in her local communities and has served as a director on the Board of Directors for the Dexter Chamber of Commerce in Missouri, as well as secretary/treasurer for the last three years. She also volunteers at different events in the surrounding area.

In her spare time, Tiffany enjoys spending time with her husband, twelve-year-old son Ryker, and their two dogs. They enjoy going on walks in the country and listening to music together. She also runs Tiffany-WrightCo, an online vintage shop specializing in vintage dishes and décor.

Kelley Lampe

I Didn't Die

I was terrified to stand and speak in front of a room of people. Being a successful sales rep, I was often asked to talk about success stories during our sales meetings. I would do anything to get out of it. I even called in sick one day because I was scheduled to make a presentation. I was in telephone sales for years, and I think I stayed there so long because it was more comfortable for me to talk on the phone rather than in person.

One day we were asked to take a personality test that was administered by an outside vendor. Several weeks later, forty of us met at the corporate office with that vendor to discuss our group's results. They called my name and asked me to leave the room. I was horrified; everyone's eyes were on me as I walked out. What was going on? After about five minutes, they asked me to come back and stand by a full-length mirror at the front of the room. The vendor said, "Tell us what you see." I froze and felt super self-conscious. I couldn't speak. The presenter asked the group what they noticed about me, and they discussed my body language and how I was "closed down." He said, "Of all the people in this room, she scored the highest in stage fright." I have never felt so exposed. I knew I had an issue with public speaking but wasn't expecting to be the one with the worst fear in the entire group. My competitive nature kicked in, like a switch was triggered in me, and I decided to find a way to be better. When I finally sat down, I said to myself, "You didn't die. Everything is OK."

This became my mantra: "I did that, and I didn't die." I am not going to lie, it was so hard. Some days were just horrible, but I just kept going. I stopped avoiding giving presentations. I grew more and more comfortable speaking. I was often asked to help mentor new reps, and I was fine one-on-one. Groups were always my challenge. When I was asked to apply for a Sales Trainer role, I was scared to death but applied and was offered the job. Again, each day I would complete a training and remind myself that I didn't die. It seemed to get easier and easier.

Along with public speaking, another thing I hated was networking. Walking into a room full of people who I didn't know and introducing myself made me anxious and uncomfortable. I avoided it at all costs. Because I had been in the same city almost my entire life, and with the same company for many years, I didn't need to network. My clients referred prospects to me, and I had lifelong connections that were good referral sources as well.

All that changed when I met my now husband, who is from St. Louis, Missouri. When we got engaged, it made more sense for me to move there because he had children in school and all their friends and family were there. So I did something that I never thought I would do—I left Texas and moved to Missouri.

I left behind my entire family and friends who I had known for years. I also left all my clients and professional connections. When I arrived in St. Louis, I only knew my fiancé and his family, and I had zero professional connections. New bonus family, new friends. I had to start all over. New everything.

Starting over meant not only learning a new city but also a new job in an industry that I had never worked in before. I started my new role as a Business Advisor in an established office where one rep had been there for more than twenty-two years and another sixteen years. Their networks were deep, and they were highly connected. I reverted to my old days where cold calling was successful for me, yet I struggled to set appointments. There was another successful rep who had been there a short time, and she got most of her appointments over LinkedIn. I tried this approach and had little to no success at that either. I was doing everything—except networking—because I hated it so much. What worked so well for others ultimately didn't work for me.

I saw the top people in my office not making cold calls and not reaching out on LinkedIn for prospecting. They didn't need to. They were getting referrals. I considered what was the fastest way to get from where I was (which was nowhere) to where they were. I needed to find how to work smarter and not harder. I needed to get out and connect with people as fast as I could, but in a way that was authentically me. That old fear rushed back in again. I hated networking, but I was going to have to force myself to do it. I felt self-conscious about meeting new people and was filled with self-doubt. I felt ill at the prospect of attending large networking events where I knew no one. I was struggling.

One of my company mentors hosted coffee meetings a few times a week to network with people. He invited me to ride along. He started the meetings by learning more about the person and what they did. He asked questions about the company they worked for and their role and who were good connections for them to meet. He offered to introduce them to people he knew. He never talked about our company, but inevitably they would ask, "And what do you do?" He would then tell them about the company and what we do to help businesses grow. If they'd ask who he needed to connect with, he had four or five people written down from their LinkedIn Connections that he would ask for an introduction. After the meeting, he always followed that up with an email and email introductions to the promised connections.

After that first coffee meeting, I knew this was a way to network that was comfortable for me and authentic to who I am. When I'd reach out to a new contact, I started my messages by saying, "I moved here from Texas and left behind my entire professional network. I would love to buy you coffee and learn more about you and who might be valuable connections for you. I am meeting a lot of people, and I would love to be able to make some introductions back to you when it makes sense to do so. Please let me know if you have some available time in the next week or two. I look forward to meeting you."

The response to these messages was incredible. Everyone who responded said "yes." I met at least three days a week for coffee or for lunch, made some amazing connections, and some became clients. I've joined a few professional women's organizations and have built an expansive network here in St. Louis.

An organization from Illinois that was looking to expand into Missouri contacted me. They said they had heard that I was one of the "go-to" people in St Louis who could make valuable connections for them in the area. I laughed to myself, knowing how much I hated networking and how far I had come in a short amount of time. Going from knowing hardly anyone here to being one of the "go-to" people.

If, on the day that I was standing in front of that mirror, you'd asked if I would be able to make meaningful connections and build a large network in a city I had never been to in my life, I would have told you, "There isn't a chance." I often think about how I got from that point to where I am today. What keeps coming back to me is "I Didn't Die." That phrase is what resilience means to me because it helped me through so many different situations, and I have grown so much because of it.

If you're trying to build your network in a way that's authentic to you:

6. Find a way to connect with people that suits you and your personality and communication style.

7. Be yourself when connecting with others. I made sure that people knew that I wasn't from here, and that I was building my professional network and would appreciate their guidance and suggestions.

8. When networking, make it about them and not you. Tell them you are happy to share connections with them when it makes sense to do so, and then do it. They will ask about you and what you do and how they can help.

9. If there is something (like stage fright) that is holding you back, start by doing something small and tell yourself "I Didn't Die." Eventually, you will be moving in directions that you never thought were possible.

Kelley Lampe is a Business Advisor and people connector. She has more than thirty-five years of experience assisting businesses to become more profitable. Many of those years were spent in advertising, and she is currently in human capital management. She has received multiple sales awards over the years for exceeding goals, including several that were awarded for long-term consistency. She attributes this to remaining focused on the needs of her clients and having a plan for each day.

Kelley is passionate about taking care of her clients and providing them with the assistance they need so they can focus on their business and improve their growth and profitability.

Kelley is originally from the Dallas/Ft. Worth, Texas, area, but currently lives in St. Louis with her husband, Paul. She is the proud bonus mom to Andrew and Sarah. Kelley enjoys traveling, and spending time with family and their pups, Mia and Sophie.

Marci Fine

Perspective

Seventeen years into my career, I was working at one of the largest advertising agencies in town. I advanced the corporate ladder and was managing a media department of more than ten people and millions of dollars in advertising for large-scale clients. I felt accomplished and had arrived by most people's standards. Yet I was unsatisfied and burnt out. I was too far removed from the aspects of the job that were once thrilling, and I was floundering. I missed the banter of the negotiation process and putting the pieces of the puzzle together that it takes to bring a media plan to fruition. I had no desire to continue along this path and no idea what I wanted to do next. A friend suggested I move into a media sales role. What a brilliant idea, I thought. So I pursued and secured a job at a local television station. It would be fulfilling. It would be in the same industry, the same lingo, just on the other side of the proverbial desk.

Only it wasn't.

I wasn't prepared for the level of transition. I thought my years of media buying would help me slide easily into this new role in media sales. What I didn't understand is what it takes to be a "seller." I worked well with my advertising agency clients, but that was transactional business, not selling. I was struggling to communicate with people who didn't know the industry lingo. Only it didn't feel like a learning curve or a gap

I had to address. It showed up like a personal failure and insufficiency. A decades-old internal dialogue of not being good enough or having what it takes came flooding in.

In a few short months, the opportunity I hoped would be exciting and revitalizing became tedious and torturous. I was filled with doubt and regret for making the change. Week after week in our sales department meetings, our individual results were projected onto the wall. I consistently ranked seventh or eighth out of eight salespeople, and my confidence couldn't have been lower. I thought about leaving, and yet I stayed.

About two years in, I had a realization as I drove to work. It was a Monday morning, and I'd taken a personal development course over the weekend. My realization was this: I could continue suffering by focusing on all the ways I felt insufficient, or I could focus on where I was having success and work on growing my knowledge. The truth was, I was earning a decent income in a commissioned sales role, so I had to be doing *something* right. In that moment I found my resilience. Sitting at my desk, I saw my space with new eyes. To my right were all my client files, and there were many. To my left was a stack of magazines and newspaper clippings with new business leads—the ones I'd avoided pursuing because I might mess up and lose the opportunity. Then I remembered the saying, "You miss 100 percent of the shots you don't take." I'd spent the last two years so bogged down by fear of failing that I hadn't taken the shots and yet somehow thought I should still be scoring.

This was also the day I defined what a seller is to me. I let go of all my preconceived notions and created the role of someone who listens to the needs of their clients and helps them achieve their objectives. It's being authentic, curious, communicative, solution-based, and of service. Now *that* was a way of being a seller I could embrace. Suddenly, I was in the same job but in a whole new world. Within the next three months, I moved up to fifth in the sales rankings, but more importantly I enjoyed what I was doing and had a sense of purpose. With resilience, I turned what was a disappointing career transition into meaningful work serving my clients.

Resilience has continued to serve me well through other professional and personal scenarios. In 2019, my dad's kidneys began to fail. He'd had chronic kidney disease for more than twenty years, and while there had been a slow decline in function during that time, it had remained high enough to support him. Then, at seventy-five years of age, it dropped drastically, and he needed a transplant. We were shocked. We were told it wasn't likely he'd receive one from the national list due to his age, even though he was in outstanding health otherwise. We needed to find a personal donor.

I wanted to be his donor and couldn't think of a better way to show my love and gratitude to my dad. Giving him back his health was something I could do for both my parents. They have always been there for me, and gave me the foundation and opportunities to build an amazing life. So, on February 26, 2020, I started the donor testing process. I was hopeful and scared, because I'd heard it was a long and painful recovery for the donor (it's not!), and because the first cases of what would become a global pandemic were reported in the United States that very same day. I worried about how this health crisis would affect my dad and the donation process, and with good reason—it brought it to a halt. The hospital focused on treating pandemic patients, and the testing process stopped.

Again, I called on my resilience to navigate this challenging time. The world was at the beginning of a pandemic and my family was dealing with my dad's failing health. There was so much to learn and so many decisions to make at a time when normal life was disrupted. To help us get through, we set up regular video chats and had dinners together from our respective tables. We talked about what we'd done that day and how we'd handle it if we had to leave the security of our houses to go out. In June of 2020, I was able to resume testing, but his kidney function had dropped into the teens. He was constantly chilly and had brain fog from the toxins in his body. He couldn't wait any longer for a donor. As my parents worked with his doctors to begin dialysis, I focused on helping them stay positive and empowered—to be present to their own resilience.

The next opportunity to be resilient came in mid-June of that year when I learned I couldn't be a donor because I have low kidney function too. Then my mom was declined as a donor. We were back at square one. The good news was he was responding well to dialysis and the situation wasn't as urgent. New people began the donor testing process, including friends, a neighbor, and even a colleague of mine I hadn't worked with in more than fifteen years. My brother ended up being a match and donated a kidney to our dad in January of 2021. I am, and will be, forever grateful. Today, they are both vibrant and in great health.

What I've learned about being resilient is that it's a choice, in every moment and every situation where I feel worn down or deflated. I have a say in what happens next—not always in the circumstances, but in how I approach them. And to be clear, I'm not talking about "pulling myself up by my bootstraps." For example, as women, I believe we're taught to power through tough situations and focus more on the doing than the being, often to the detriment of our physical and emotional well-being. I've sometimes heard, and always disliked, the expression "God doesn't give us more than we can handle." I don't believe that expression, regardless of whether you believe in God, the Universe, a Higher Power, or that it's just the circumstances you've been dealt. However, I recently heard someone say "God doesn't give us more than we can handle, with help." Now that's an idea I can get behind.

Resilience, the capacity to recover quickly from difficulties, is something each and every one of us has. What I've learned through my experiences is that when I can't tap into it on my own, it's time to turn to those around me for help.

Marci Fine is a marketing and media consultant with more than thirty years' experience advising agencies and brands. As the Midwest representative for Q1Media, an Austin-based digital media services company, she brings a strategic and enthusiastic approach to helping clients. She is a member of the Sponsorship committee for 314Digital and was a former board member for Fathers' Support Center and Explore Transplant. Marci graduated from the National Council of Jewish Women leadership training course and has participated in leadership and self-development training for more than a decade as Introduction Leader for Landmark Education.

Marci holds a dual degree in Journalism and Sociology from Indiana University in Bloomington, Indiana. She and her wife, Laura, live in St. Louis with their three fur babies, Mia, Gabby, and Willow. She enjoys spending quality time with family and friends, puzzling, traveling, fashion, and checking out the latest dining opportunities in St. Louis.

Tracy Tubbesing

Break the Chains

What is the key to happiness? My entire personal and professional life had been based on society's perspective and I was thriving! Breaking the glass ceiling, surrounding myself with family and friends, finding my life partner, becoming an entrepreneur, building a beautiful home, and bringing the best versions of ourselves into the world with two incredible boys. Life threw curveballs, however; nothing could stop us from building our empire. At least that is what I thought.

SELF-AWARENESS

The pressure of my career as an HR executive, pursuing my bachelor's degree, caring for our children, nurturing relationships, and life itself became layers upon layers of stress. My ability to endure stress and excel was at a robotic level. However, in the blink of an eye I found myself in survival mode. My body reached a breaking point resulting in a grand mal seizure. The aftermath from loss of consciousness and abnormal electrical activity to my brain far exceeded anything I could ever imagine. Life as I knew it was never the same. I was drifting farther and farther away each day from the shining light of my life and into the darkness. I did not even recognize myself in the mirror as the sparkle in my eyes went blank.

My years of stresses were many: trauma from my seizure; financial hardship of losing my job as a result of the pandemic; uncertainty of the future; losing my sense of identity; grief from the loss of my dear great-grandma, my grandmother, grandfather, and other loved ones; the tragedy of losing my brother-in-law to suicide; rejection from my biological father; facing the judgement of my male colleagues for disrupting the status quo as a woman at the senior leadership table; navigating my children through hardships; and pressures to present an image of perfection to the world. I felt tangled in chains, suffocating from the pain and unable to breathe. The links were intertwined with toxic people, unhealthy habits, lack of self-love, overwhelming self-doubt, trauma, grief, tragedies, rejection, anxiety, depression, career, living under others' thumbs and demands, and the strongest link—my brain. My strength of resilience was at full force trying to elevate me and my superwoman powers.

The elevation level soared to an inability to take in oxygen. This was a pivotal point—my first panic attack. My body was deteriorating physically and emotionally. The chains tightened around me as I was becoming a prisoner in my own body. Oh, the pain ran deep. Living in the dark, surrounded by four walls, finding comfort cuddling with the only friend I had at that moment, my best furry friend, Bella. She gave me unconditional love with no judgement, with her ears perked up, ready to listen and always with a spirit of joy. Bella passed unexpectedly, and my soul was empty. This was my First Pillar of Resilience: recognizing my Self-Awareness of hopelessness. My light started to dim.

MINDFULNESS

What happened to me? I was not in a good headspace and my anxiety disabled me from doing daily basic tasks. I hid behind my smile and was an imposter of happiness. The chains became heavier and sharper, digging into my skin. My mindfulness pushed me to see my doctor. I was diagnosed with major depressive disorder. No mirrors, please … I hated her . . . I resented her . . . so I started to hide my "real." I isolated from everyone and made excuses to not attend events as I could not risk being exposed. The side effects of the medication, isolation, rejections from a hard job economy, and damaging relationships all spiraled me into a deep depressive state.

Medicine numbed my pain and helped me pass the hours of the day. Loved ones tried everything to save me and they felt helpless. After all, how could they help me when I did not want to be saved? It was a constant pull-push with everyone. My mind was racing 24/7 with negative thoughts of self-doubt, shaking my confidence and self-worth. This was fear filled with lies. It became my truth, however. I was beautifully broken and a mess of chaos. Demons I never knew surfaced from my core and disrupted my peace. I so desperately needed to get out of the dark and into the light. Sadly, I wanted nothing more than to be invisible and disappear. Then it hit me like a brick wall. My adult children could no longer bear the agony of my suffering, wondering if their mom was every going to come back. This was my "light bulb" moment, and my Second Pillar of Resilience: Mindfulness.

SELF CARE

Tuning into my body was at a critical state. It was time to surrender and take control of my health. My first step: gather extensive knowledge of the brain and depression. By the grace of God, I was guided to Greenbrook NeuroHealth Centers where I was educated on TMS Therapy (Transcranial Magnetic Stimulation Therapy). This was a huge milestone in my journey to healing. After thirty-six treatments, it worked! I walked away from depression and never looked back. I also committed to talk therapy and learned I never truly loved myself. I finally understood the meaning of self-love, and my inability to be able to be present for anyone until I started to nurture and love myself.

This was my Third Pillar of Resilience: Self-Care—the power and strength of self-love ripped off the tremendous weights of the chains I felt I was carrying, and I became freer each day. I replaced my bed for exercise, my medicine for affirmations, my worry with meditations, journaling, inspirational speakers, choosing a tribe with higher expectations of character, and traded isolation for spending time with family and friends. My bravest move: saying "Yes" to Jennifer Bardot when asked to author a chapter in her analogy book, *Resilience*. Sharing my story with the world has helped me heal, and it's my hope it will help others hurting in silence. You are not alone. You are worthy. I truly believe the ones hurting are the best healers. The world simply needs kindness. Smile often, do small gestures of kindness, and check in on others.

PURPOSE

The pandemic allowed me to reflect on my life, and now with a clear mind I took a brave step back into the world of networking. With a goal to get back into the workforce, I joined a nonprofit group offering engagements for career opportunities through networking. My natural ability to connect with people did not go unnoticed. Within a few months, I was elected as president on the board of directors. This was a huge honor! It provided me the opportunity to give back to the community and share my story. It gave me a sense of identity and a higher purpose than I could ever imagine. Fulfilling the mission to help the St. Louis Community was part of my "light" out of the "darkness." I was finally starting to feel happiness. So much so, I put my job search on hold to help those less fortunate.

The partnerships, the healthy environment, the empowerment— these all contributed to breaking off the remaining pieces of chain links holding me back from my full potential. The Fourth Pillar of Resilience validates the advice to "trust the process," and shines a star so bright that it can only come from a higher power. I finally understood the reason for my journey. This path was created for me to learn valuable life lessons, to regain my spirituality, to give hope to those in need, to find my purpose, and most importantly to find my inner happiness and love myself!

Resilience is strength to bend, not break. It is rooted in a desire for survival, nurtured by the collective support of others. Each of the Four Pillars of Resilience in my journey taught me lessons I could have never learned without traveling the bumpy and dirty road. I was resourceful by building resilience to identify the right tools for me personally. Once my energy and perspective shifted to positive mode, my path was clear, and I was finally free.

Leaning into resilience and to those who rooted for my rise is irreplaceable. I will forever be grateful to those who stood firmly by my side, surrounding me with silent prayers, unconditional love, nonjudgement, belief, and navigating me to my purpose. Words will never be enough to thank those who saved me from taking away the beautiful gift of life my mom chose for me decades ago. Today, I proudly accept this gift back with open arms of gratitude and grace. I am no longer my depression. I am no longer my fear. I am no longer my anxiety. I bravely shine my light for everybody to see. I am Tracy. And I will forever choose myself first. The chain I felt tortured by for many years was my protector to keep me grounded so I could live my life to the fullest and serve my *purpose* to the world!

Tracy Tubbesing is VP of Human Resources at Brand Addition. She is an HR executive with an extensive generalist background in the global private and public sectors. Tracy is highly skilled in organizational transformations and orchestrating rapid business growth through a multitude of acquisitions. Tracy has stamped her name in the industry as a strategic business partner and trusted advisor providing HR expertise and business solutions.

Tracy's passion is people! She pours her heart into her work and leaves a little sparkle wherever she goes. Tracy was awarded Manager of the Year during her tenure with TricorBraun.

Tracy serves on the board of directors for Job Seekers' Garden Club and also volunteers for a number of local nonprofit organizations. Tracy is a member of the Lewis & Clark SHRM chapter, RAD Networking, AAIM, and the National HR Association.

Tracy earned her BA in Human Resources Management from Lindenwood University.

Sheila Pride

Wounded Healer to Sacred Warrior

One message from my culture I received early on was that God/Spirit was external to me and something to be feared. Attending church, reciting prayers, confession, and rigid rules about divorce, remarriage, and sexual orientation felt unloving. My eight-year-old self knew that cloud gazing, dancing barefoot, and collapsing under a giant oak tree with my belly and heart pressing on the earth connected me to something bigger.

I would later discover myself to be an extreme empath or highly sensitive person. I felt the suffering of others inside my body, and I was committed to liberating myself and others from that shared pain, even at an early age.

My childhood was a perfect training ground for my hero's journey and my life's work of trauma healing, advocacy, and empowerment. My early days were marked with the blessings of an extended family, a magnificent rural landscape, hard physical work, softball grit, and the love of an imperfect family. Unknowingly at the time, many of my family members, including my beloved grandparents, had experienced significant trauma and soul loss that was being passed down. None of us had healthy coping mechanisms, but we were doing our best. We all collectively witnessed and/or experienced violence, relational dysregulation, and addiction.

When I was twelve years old, my parents separated, making space for new characters who would influence our development, giving pause to escalating dysregulated dynamics. It took a few years of difficult experiences, but my family had the transformation it needed. For me, moving to the city, changing schools repeatedly, sexual harassment, loss of nature, and my sibling's fall into a methamphetamine addiction were chiseling forces that created long-lasting imprints.

I found belonging by helping and serving others. I joined peer counseling, tutoring, sports, and charity events. These inherent experiences shaped my future choice to be a social worker in human rights. Like many others, my early wounds drove me to help others. I was on fire to change the system and fight for others. It felt good to access my inner warrior and create change. As social workers, our motto was if you are not outraged, you are not paying attention! That motto took its toll on my health and relationships. I ruined countless Thanksgiving dinners and casual conversations meant for connection. I lacked tolerance and compassion for those with opposing values or who hadn't shed their mindset of privilege. I experienced internalized shame and guilt for belonging to a majority group responsible for oppression. I used shame as a strategy to get people to change or to retaliate when I felt condemned to hell for helping Muslims and advocating for LGBTQ persons. Over time I lost my religion, roots, and my most important need, a connection to Spirit.

Unknowingly, I had sidestepped my healing process and deepened my unresolved trauma by working in high-risk and high-stress conditions with little time for self-care or joy. My filters changed, making it harder to see the beauty around me. I was not resilient, and I had full-blown PTSD from what I saw every day in our community.

After eight years of working with high caseloads in the field of violence and abuse, I became very sick. I developed fibromyalgia and Epstein-Barr at the age of twenty-eight. Fear was ever-present and heightened to an unbearable level with the birth of my firstborn daughter. I had to transform; I wanted to be healthy for myself and mostly for my daughter. I wanted to see the world and the people in it as beautiful again.

When reality hit that I would have to change my profession so I could heal, I felt despair and falsely believed my life had no value if I wasn't helping others in extreme situations. At that moment, I realized I had abandoned myself.

Over the next five years, I embarked on a resiliency journey that would change me from the inside out. I worked with mind/body/spirit medicine and climbed through the anxieties of illness and divorce into a full recovery. I remembered how nature was my main portal to spiritual renewal. I evolved my meaning of resiliency to be more than getting back on the horse. I learned to pivot and heal my attachment wounds, communicate with more love, and improve relational dynamics. I immersed myself in studying Eastern healing. I became a yoga and qigong teacher and somatic therapist. I began practicing my coaching work in an integrated way. I had a second child, a son, who helped me heal the wounds of the masculine. I began to find ways to bring resiliency into every aspect of my life.

I learned to self-regulate and to avoid the typical empath over-care to depletion pattern. This was the biggest leap I had to take. I now maintain resiliency through the regular practice of yoga, HeartMath, and bodywork.

My resiliency is also heightened by having a spiritual community that matches my soul's need for embodied nature practices. With help, I learned to feel Spirit and my ancestors always supporting me. I learned to practice prayer in a different way that felt right in my bones. I am honored to have been embraced by my mentors: First Nation Elder Sharon Oxendine, and

Shamanic Healer Suzannah Tebbe Davis. They have been critical in my resiliency journey.

My heart's work continues today, and training resiliency and coherence is a core principle of it.

I cofounded The Moksha Group more than ten years ago with my husband, Ryan Pride. We work globally supporting leaders, teams, and everyday people to awaken from suffering and to find more joy. We work with schools, hospitals, small businesses, and billion-dollar companies. It doesn't matter where we go, we find that people are hungry for deep, meaningful connection, ease from their suffering, healing of their patterns, and practices that will help them show up at their best for those that mean the most.

At Moksha we share ancient wisdom practices for our modern times. Most recently, we started an inspiring podcast called *Leading from the Heart*. Check us out on YouTube and at mokshagroup.com.

Sheila Renee Pride, LCSW, RYT, LMT is the CEO of the Moksha Group. She is a business consultant and heart-based change agent—leading transformation for leaders, teams, and organizations across the country. Sheila applies neuroscience and leverages contemplative practice tools and techniques to create meaningful change. In addition to fifteen years of clinical experience as a therapist, social worker, and trauma recovery advocate, Sheila is also a certified practitioner in many energy sciences: yoga, qigong, SER (somatic release), and biofeedback therapies.

Sheila's consultation/training/coaching is designed to awaken the heart and soul of a leader and an organization—moving into healing so they can lead with an internal feeling of steadiness, discernment, and joy and empower those around them. She is grateful for her rural roots and urban life. She loves horses, djembe, nature, and dancing. She has two amazing children and an amazing partner in work and life.

Sonia Westburg

No Expiration Date

I have always wanted to be self-employed. But, as a young parent, I didn't have the financial means to take the risk while raising my three sons. While the desire was there, I needed a steady paycheck to raise my family. Here's my story of how what looked like a major setback in my life turned into an opportunity to run my own business. Through determination and a resilient spirit, I made it happen.

In April 2017, I found out when I returned from lunch on a Friday that I was unemployed *again*. Completely out of left field. It's happened a few times over my career history, but this time I was working in a government position and had been reassured many times that this position was set until I was ready to retire.

I was forty-nine, and my youngest son was a fourteen-year-old in junior high. My two eldest sons had already left the nest and were living independently in another state. We were living in a smaller community with few job prospects. I was one week away from closing on the dream house I'd wanted for years. I frantically tried to figure out if we should stay in the area and buy the house and just hope it all worked out, or if I should pull out of the contract and continue renting to have the flexibility to move if needed for a new job. With a heavy heart, I pulled out of the contract. With hope, fingers crossed, and prudent living, we would pull through financially.

August 2017. I had not been feeling well for several months before and during all this but had assumed it was due to the high stress of my job and then unemployment. I've had an ongoing history of autoimmune diseases since high school and acquired more complications as I got older.

My youngest son mentioned that the whites of my eyes were extremely yellow and wanted to know if I was OK. A visit to my doctor the next morning became an emergency admittance to the hospital and a flurry of testing. I was diagnosed with complete liver failure and was told that I'd most likely never leave the hospital to return home. I have faced extreme medical issues several times before. But the doctors had always offered me hope as they discussed my medical options. This time was different. I wasn't being offered hope or medical options from any of the doctors who stopped by my hospital room and tried to figure out what was going on. I was told to make my final arrangements, that time was not on my side. I knew I didn't feel well, but I certainly didn't feel that it was the "end" yet!

I am fortunate to live in the "right" time of medicine and to live close to Memphis, Tennessee, where the specialist who diagnosed my latest disease is based. If this had happened more than ten to fifteen years ago, I wouldn't be here today. It is only within that time frame that modern medicine realized that autoimmune hepatitis can be managed with daily medications for a limited amount of time. There is no answer for why my body stopped working as it should. It's not something I caught from someone else, and it's not hereditary. There is no cure for autoimmune hepatitis. It can only be managed with a daily medication regimen that allows my body to keep my liver enzymes in check. The medications have their own set of issues and side effects. However, my system has been thrown off to the point that, in addition to all my other medical issues, I am now diabetic.

I will admit, being diagnosed as a diabetic was extremely difficult for me to mentally accept. I struggled for about six months to accept my new reality. I can't say why this diagnosis was so hard to accept. I have certainly faced much worse. Once I was able to accept that this was part of my new normal and became compliant in taking insulin, I started to feel much better. I am not cured. Following my doctors' recommendations "buys" me time and allows me to be here to see my youngest son graduate school in May 2023 (and hopefully college after that). It has allowed me the time to be here to see my two older sons get married and to welcome my two granddaughters into this world.

Due to the long recovery, I realized that I am no longer able to work a standard job, so it was the right time to strike out and become my own boss. I worked part time as a substitute teacher while I started my business as a Loan Signing Agent/Mobile Notary. Within a year I took the leap to working full time for myself. Being self-employed allows me to spend more time with my sons and granddaughters, and to travel more. I remind myself daily of the grace and many blessings I have been given.

My Resilience: It can be difficult to see the path when you are in the middle of it. By no means is my journey complete. I do feel that each step in my career prepared me to be successful when I became my own boss. Looking back, I can see where I gained the knowledge, experience, and drive to strike out on my own, even when so many people around me were naysayers, telling me that I needed to quit playing and get a real job. Is it scary? Oh my goodness, yes! Even now, it's scary. Because I don't get a paycheck for just showing up. I must work every day to maintain and build my business connections, stay focused, and be prepared. Today's mortgage market and higher interest rates have changed the flow of my business. To me, it means I buckle down and work harder. I won't give up. I am resilient.

My Key Takeaways:

10. Set goals, stay fluid, be ready to pivot. To be self-employed, you usually can't be set in your ways.

11. Learn from others, whether their behaviors are good or bad. Most of the time you learn more from the mistakes or bad behaviors of others by correcting or not making them yourself.

12. Have faith, trust your instincts, and believe in yourself. Repeat this as many times as you need to in regard to your professional and personal life.

I'm still here. Some days are physically harder than others. Some say it's because I'm a fighter—that's probably true. I say it's because I'm not ready yet and there is so much more I want to do, see, and experience. And most importantly, there is no expiration date stamped on the bottom of my foot.

Sonia (Schoonover) Westburg is a Montana native residing in Arkansas. She has built a successful mobile notary/signing agent business. She has a passion to share her knowledge and support with the notary community.

In addition to running her business, she is an Arkansas-assigned state mentor offering education to commissioned notaries, providing an opportunity for notaries to increase their knowledge of state-specific notarial law, rules, and regulations.

Sonia is a proud mother of three grown sons. As a former Navy wife, she has had careers mainly focusing on HR and paralegal work. She is starting a new adventure recording voice-over work. Her voice can already be heard on voicemail systems across the USA. She is looking forward to recording her first audiobook.

Sonia enjoys cruising the world (one island at a time) with her partner, Robert Lowe, and experiencing adventures with her sister, Shannon.

Shannon Stanfield

Putting the Pieces Together

Life brings challenges. Many of us power through and take necessary steps to reach our goals, passions, and desires. Yet we don't often reflect on our uniqueness and our story. People have told me that I'm strong in tough situations. My first thought is to reply, "Anyone would do the same." I have discovered that, often, this is not the case.

In all situations, I try to see the bigger picture and weigh the pluses and minuses. My ability to be analytical helped form this perspective. I find it difficult to step back and view myself from another's perspective. Yet when we take that moment and look deeply enough, we may see different versions of ourselves in each person. When all the pieces are put together, we discover our legacy. There is a proverb I often think of: "The biggest troublemaker you will have to deal with watches you from the mirror every morning." The truth is, each of us will determine how we react to circumstances and how we allow things to affect us. One lesson I have learned in life is that when negative things happen, sometimes the situation is a lesson for us. Often, it is how we overcome the situation that teaches others how to persevere and move forward.

As a child I learned early to depend on myself and work hard. I haven't viewed my life any other way. My strength and drive came from the thought of moving forward without help. If something needed to be done, I needed to act. A defining time in my life began in 2002. I worked for one of the largest credit card companies in the world. I was offered a promotion in Virginia while I was going through a divorce. I reviewed the logistics of moving and made the decision. My children and I began a new step in our journey.

Challenges and obstacles presented themselves in Virginia, and I had second thoughts about the move. The job required travel and I didn't have resources in the area. I sent my children to North Carolina to live with my sister Sonia while I figured it out. I felt like I made a mistake. Eventually, I knew I made the right decision when things began to fall into place. Sonia even moved to Richmond. Life was beautiful. Then, something I never saw coming gave me the ultimate challenge to my resilience and self-reliance.

I went to Vietnam for ten days on vacation. When I returned, I jumped back into work and was on the verge of making my last car payment. Five days before Christmas, my normally uneventful drive home from work became eventful. I was driving down the freeway, and suddenly a car came in my direction. I quickly said, "God, take care of my kids." The first impact on the driver's side exploded my airbag. My world went dark. Driven by a teenager, the other car went on to hit me two more times, and my car went off the road and rolled three times. When I came to, my car was facing the road and I saw cars slowly pass by. The stereo was blaring, and even with the pain, I was embarrassed. I reached over to turn it off, and a voice from the back seat said, "Don't move." The voice came from a paramedic who was holding my neck. I was in shock.

Fortunately, the next exit was the exit for the hospital. It was shift change, and drivers who witnessed the accident worked at the hospital. I panicked when I realized that my children needed to be picked up. Someone called Sonia and explained that they were waiting for transport and for the Jaws of Life to release me from the car. The roof of the car was touching the top of my head, and I had dirt and sticks wedged in my nostrils.

My next thought was, "Where is my work computer? I have urgent work to do tonight." I joked about losing my job if I missed my deadline. But "That's okay," I said, "because my next career could be as a crash test dummy." I am pretty good at surviving major accidents. I told a few off-color jokes, and my faceless paramedic laughed and asked if I was a comedian. It was his job to keep my spirits up. He told me I had rolled down my window even though it was raining. I didn't know why I had done that since it was a manual window. My face was saved from being severely cut during the accident because the window had been open. All the glass broke inside the door on impact. I have never met this man, but he was my angel that day, and I will never forget him.

I was transported to the hospital, where I demanded that we call my manager before undergoing X-rays. I didn't back down, so the doctor relented. My manager was in a team meeting that I had not attended due to being on vacation and was shocked at my call. He assured me not to worry, he would take care of everything.

After leaving the hospital, I couldn't move my left hand and had zero feeling in my fingers. Sonia took me to the scrap yard to recover my personal items from the car. The man who towed my car started out by giving us his condolences, as he thought the driver had been killed. He was incredulous that I had survived, and said it took hours to clean up the accident debris. Then, we discovered that my purse was missing. Another obstacle had presented itself.

That evening after leaving the scrap yard, I received a call with the news that the client party I had been planning on attending had been cancelled. "Some idiot rolled their car and backed up traffic for hours," they said. I got a kick out of explaining that I was the idiot. I assured them I was fine and secured a ride to work from my client since I would be able to return immediately.

Then, another miracle happened. My divorce would be finalized in January, and by law I wasn't allowed to purchase anything before it was. I received a random call from a dealership asking if I needed a car. I explained the situation to them, and they picked me up. When we arrived at the dealership, I noticed a sign that read, "God provides." I felt at peace and had the best car buying experience I'd ever had. They offered me the car for a month until my divorce finalized. I am amazed that the dealership offered this.

During my recovery, I encountered physical limitations that called for creative solutions. I couldn't hold a book, for example. Many other struggles presented themselves, but I learned to adapt. I began hand therapy three times a week. I was determined to use my hand and regain what I had lost. Progress was slow, and when people commented on how awful it was, I would say, "I am alive. If I was half an inch taller, I wouldn't be here today."

Progress was slow. Feelings in my hand started to return along with pain. I gained the ability move some fingers, except my middle one. My sons were delighted. They laughed over people who were upset, thinking I was giving them the finger. My recovery became about finding humor, joy, and lightness. During this time, I remembered I am a living example for my children. I went back to work after my accident and didn't let anything hold me back. I had surgery seven years later, which has eased some of the limitations and pain. It will be a small struggle for the rest of my life.

The company moved me back to Phoenix ten months after the accident. Four months later I was promoted and moved back to Virginia.

Five months later I was relocated to Pennsylvania. It was at that moment that I knew I was a warrior. I had survived this accident and moved cross country four times as a single mom in four years while traveling extensively for work. I learned that I am the only thing that can hold me back. Attitude and approach make the difference.

My car accident and recovery taught me that when an obstacle is in your path, if you find the passion and resilience to overcome it, you are unstoppable. Looking at the bigger picture, overcoming obstacles means taking steps instead of focusing on sorrow. When we reflect on our journey, we often want to change something. There isn't anything I would change about my story. Changing one experience would change me, my life, and the people who are with me for the ride. Some were there for the entire ride, and others for a moment. In life, when we are dealt a bad card, it isn't about us; it's about teaching others to handle similar situations with joy. When we realize that difficult circumstances handled with resilience create growth for ourselves or for people our story touches, that is when we truly understand the bigger picture. When life hits hard, fight back, maintain an attitude of gratitude, take a moment to breathe, and move forward.

Shannon Stanfield is an accomplished executive with more than twenty-five years of experience in business development and B2B relationship management within the payment industry. Her career includes a rich background delivering impressive results within global financial services, as well as national nonprofit, private sector, and public sector clients. This vast range of experience has given Shannon the unique ability to understand and appreciate distinct and disparate environments while focusing on transforming strategic goals into actions.

Shannon takes pride in ensuring her clients receive exceptional products and services. She is dedicated to assisting her clients with managing, auditing, and growing extensive P-Card programs and Virtual Payment Accounts.

Shannon is passionate about animals and nature. In her free time, she enjoys experiencing new adventures, gardening, traveling, and spending time with her husband, four children, and her daughter-in-law.

WOMEN OF

SEEKING TO ENGAGE·ELEVATE·LEAD

AGCMO

ENGAGING WOMEN

AN OPPORTUNITY FOR WOMEN
IN THE CONSTRUCTION INDUSTRY
TO RECEIVE SUPPORT AND
PROFESSIONAL GROWTH
THROUGH AGCMO.

GET IN TOUCH

DENISE HASTY
dhasty@agcmo.org

CHARLYCE RUTH
cruth@agcmo.org

WOMEN OF

SEEKING
TO
ENGAGE
ELEVATE
LEAD

"Resilience is a choice. It is a choice to treat failures as experiences. It is a choice to treat failures as experiences.
It is a choice to put excuses aside, commit, be persistent, and lead with purpose."
– Jennifer Bardot

SUPER SMOKERS
BBQ + CAJUN

CATERING AND FOOD TRUCK
SERVICES FOR EVERY OCCASION!

WEDDINGS
CORPORATE EVENTS
GRADUATIONS
ANNIVERSARIES
CELEBRATION OF LIFE GATHERINGS

🌐 www.supersmokers.com

📞 636-938-9742

📍 9527 Gravois Rd, St. Louis, MO 63123
1567 W 5th Street Eureka MO 63025

OWNED BY MICHELLE FITTER - AUTHOR IN RESILIENCE

CREATE • PUBLISH • PROMOTE

Cathy Davis

CreativePublishingPartners.com

FIND YOUR VOICE • SHARE YOUR STORY • TRANSFORM THE WORLD